CYBERSECURITY

CYBERSECURITY

ISSUES OF TODAY, A PATH FOR TOMORROW

Daniel Reis

ARCHWAY
PUBLISHING

Archway Publishing books may be ordered through booksellers or by contacting:

Archway Publishing
1663 Liberty Drive
Bloomington, IN 47403
www.archwaypublishing.com
1 (888) 242-5904

Because of the dynamic nature of the Internet, any web addresses or links contained in this book may have changed since publication and may no longer be valid. The views expressed in this work are solely those of the author and do not necessarily reflect the views of the publisher, and the publisher hereby disclaims any responsibility for them.

Any people depicted in stock imagery provided by Thinkstock are models, and such images are being used for illustrative purposes only. Certain stock imagery © Thinkstock.

ISBN: 978-1-4808-3030-1 (sc)
ISBN: 978-1-4808-3031-8 (hc)
ISBN: 978-1-4808-3032-5 (e)

Library of Congress Control Number: 2016906973

Print information available on the last page.

Archway Publishing rev. date: 08/18/2016

Contents

ACKNOWLEDGEMENTS

I would like to thank my girlfriend Cindy Wood for all her support and patience with me completing an MS in Information Systems Security, and then being a glutton for punishment with the near three years to write this book. Also, I wish to thank Steve Edwards for his editing, advice on my overall writing tone, John Walker for his security and editing, and Mike Adler for taking the time to read the manuscript and provide input. All were very supportive, gracious and helpful.

Introduction

What This Book Is About

Securing our data and systems today and in the future is critical. To do this, business and technology professionals have to deal with the problems of today's security technology to maintain security now, as well as how to use it to secure systems and data against future issues. Cybersecurity's primary focus are business issues; but it has historically been driven by technical aspects that have oriented it as a technology solution instead of business oriented solution that people must continually encounter. A goal here is to provide insight into the current state of security solutions and the industry, taking into consideration the changes that need to be addressed due to current and future challenges rooted in securing computing resources and data. This includes the types of security issues organizations face today as well as threat prospects we will likely face in the foreseeable future. It's evident that securing systems and data is inherently difficult and problematic for the security industry and organizations alike. Accounting for the number of choices and nearly unlimited options for network and security design and implementation, and the sophistication of today's hackers, sometimes makes it a wonder that any protection is been as effective as it has been. Clearly there has been a tremendous amount of thought and effort to continue to move protection forward. However, the issues surrounding the complexity created by the many facets of computing and security environments are not expected to disappear anytime soon, and are continually complicating the ability to secure data. These issues are endemic to any organization that simply wants to use computing resources while also keeping its data secure. It would be nice if it was simple to succeed at protection, but it isn't.

Defining Cybersecurity[1]

Cybersecurity is an ongoing exercise applied to all the elements that make up computing devices. This includes various types of computers, smartphones, private and public network devices, the Internet, and all the devices and software comprised within the global computing sphere. This field also includes all the processes and mechanisms by which digital equipment, information, and services are allowed access and protected from unintended or unauthorized access, change, or destruction. This must include physical security, as online security, physical and digital security is intertwined. Any breach is bad; however, a physical security breach can be one of the most catastrophic kinds of security breaches because it can allow full access to both data and equipment, and is usually the result of an attack from an internal source. Overall, cyber security is the process of applying security measures in order to ensure data confidentiality, integrity, and availability (CIA) to authorized parties for information that is in transit or at rest.

The Purpose Is to Protect Core Information

An area crucial to protecting all data that needs to be considered is the need to address personal identity and personal information ownership and privacy. The question of who legally owns information about individuals within organizations is fundamental to being able to control and protect it. Without some clearly defined rules or laws to address identity information ownership, as well as rules for utilizing and sharing individual and organizational information, protecting this data will continue to be difficult, if not impossible. There are numerous regulations in the United States that cover portions of this issue, but there is nothing close to being comprehensive. In the United States, the rules for data privacy generally apply to specific industries, such as health care (HIPAA),

---

[1] Wikipedia – https://en.wikipedia.org/wiki/Computer_security Feb 2016 Portions taken from Computer Security; I have made changes to suit my purposes here.

unlike the overall privacy directives that Europeans instituted, covering all members of the European Union.

There could be a form of a "fair use" rules that allow organizations to be able to utilize personal information they gather based on their research, analysis, and ongoing business practices, without putting it at risk. For these rules to be useful, everyone needs to accept that there are different classes of information, such as details about individuals that should be treated with more control to its access and use. Organizations could have access under a system that ensures they have proper credentials and follow established procedures for personal data handling and disposition. Perhaps it could be checked out for a certain period of time for specific use in nonhuman readable format and then either returned, or it could automatically delete. Every organization that checked out data would also have to follow certain standards that show that the data's integrity was met. There could even be a liability insurance program based on an organization having met certain protection methodology benchmarks to ensure overall data compliance and provide coverage against a breach. To allay organizational concerns, knowledge learned from using personal information would not be lost; they could own the resulting data as their own intellectual property without containing or be directly tied to an individual's identity or personal information. To manage more sensitive personal information, there could be a method to anonymize that data in order to help ensure that any sensitive or personal information is left at the source or, at minimum, obfuscated when used by an organization for various purposes. This could leave personal information within the domain of its owner within a single point of storage and access control to better protect it and allow authorized organizations with access when needed. There are a number of issues if attempting to anonymize information today because as we know now there are tens of thousands of different systems that store personal information. In addition, systems and software can pretty easily correlate information from just a few of these stored systems along with the constant "data exhaust" all of us create with our online lives[2] means anyone can at some level can be identified. There are a lot of technical as well as potential legal issues to being able to protect personal data and still make it available for research or other reasonable business uses. Unfortunately, there aren't any silver-bullet answers to this problem. But the fact stands that regardless of methodology, the current level of private-information exposure; because there is no single owner a whole host of problems are created that won't go away until some type of reliable privacy ownership and control can be defined and implemented.

Establishing some type of usable system for data-privacy control could help resolve the issues created when thousands of organizations store varying amounts of both accurate and inaccurate personal information. Because there is a tremendous amount of conflicting data stored in thousands of different places, this makes data access, protection, and *data integrity* even more difficult. This fact is attested to by the many major breaches in the news every year that expose tens of millions of personal records.

With over thirty years as a business and technology professional as well as over fifteen years in computing security has provided me with many opportunities to meet and learn from thousands of small and large company's security and business professionals. I've been able to discuss many of their concerns, ranging from their current security issues and struggles as well as what they see as potential issues and a future threat landscape. This experience has permitted me to draw on a lot of smart people's knowledge, thoughtful reflection, and concerns. I hope that is reflected in this book.

---

[2] Economist Magazine, ""Data Privacy – We'll see you, anon," August 15, 2015.

My conclusion is that information security is seriously struggling to meet many of its necessary requirements. There is a constant churn of security companies and organizations working to extend their existing products or create new ones to try to address old and new security issues as well as new threat types, vulnerabilities or bugs. This continuous new product or feature flow reminds me of the proverbial elephant in the room where each company is trying to identify what they should create while only being able to identify one obscure part of the elephants body. As we've all found in developing any kind of defense against attacks, the difficulty is identifying the body part they're actually touching. At issue is that identifying aspects can be hidden because organizations have to deal with the complexity of their own environments. Then add complex attacks and tools that can only identify issues within a narrow scope or threat tunnel vision. When you then include the stealth and obfuscation used by hackers to further their aims, which also take advantage of security and network complexity as well as yet-to-be-discovered security issues, one can understand not being able to realize it's an entire elephant, not just the single point they're touching. The identity issues continue to be exacerbated by an ever-more complex and overwhelmingly active computing and security environment. All of this further blindfolds security's ability to either spot a perpetrator or chase down what they may be trying to do, or simply try to assess where a perpetrator may be in an organizations network. To further complicate this issue, not only is everyone trying to identify the elephant by touching one part at a time, but the elephant also continues to move and change position so that no one is continually touching the same point, even if someone had finally figured out the part they were touching. From a security standpoint, hackers are like dancing elephants in front of a blindfolded audience—difficult to pin down and devastatingly effective at damaging an organization as they joyously step on everything in their midst.

It is clearly difficult for any security organization or person, no matter how good it or they may be, to quickly develop a complete and overall picture of a hacker's attack, or assign attribution to any particular hacker or group. This can be made tougher as many organizations have a difficult time knowing what their ideal baseline state is for systems and security in order to help determine what took place during an attack or by who, whether their security policies and solutions were effective, how effective, or are failing and if so how. The fact is that security tends to be implemented as a reactive, groping-in-the-dark methodology to address a wide array of possible attacks, with the hope that if something is discovered (while praying nothing will be); a rapid reaction can be applied effectively to block and remediate any threat. Historically, security means a lot of broadly targeted efforts at perceived threats based on what a defender can observe with his or her limited tools. Often, their measures are a reasonable reaction to what is understood regarding a threat, but are often either too late or misaligned with the actual attack. This tendency makes sense when one realizes how difficult it is to pinpoint a threat in order to aim any protection against it, but the fact is that many responses are habitual reactions that often haven't enough clarity on an actual threat to be as effective as needed. The unfortunate reality is that just because an organization has reacted to a perceived threat doesn't mean they've moved in the best direction at that moment or for the long term. And, this reactive modus operandi doesn't scale well with the increasing complexity of security and networks or threats at large. The growth, sophistication and potential areas of threat compromises has grown exponentially, with methods and tools still primarily focused at a more knee-jerk reaction level to a narrowly defined threat picture. The issue is that reactions tend to be frequent and, unfortunately result in decreasing accuracy of protection against an actual threat. And attacks have become more systematic over the last five to ten years, to take advantage of security's tendency of continuous reaction as a foundation of their security operational mode.

This becomes an even more serious problem when each security event is reviewed as an individual occurrence. Any related events, like all the combined parts that make up the elephant in the room, can't be addressed or understood even though they pertain to an entire network with applications, devices, and traffic volume. Even though a part of the elephant—one specific event—may be addressed, the rest of it remains under a cloud of anonymity. A part of this is the continued reliance on static systems as a standard for reactive identification and remediation of threats that have been identified. At issue is that the attacks are dynamic activities, and using static tools in a fast moving environment is like tying the elephant's foot with a string and thinking it will be able to keep it from stampeding.

To actually provide the protection necessary, instead of tying string around the moving elephant's toe and hoping for the best, technicians have to spot and understand a threat as it's happening, in the context of the entire system the threat is operating within. And a part of this means they must be able to track a threat as it actively tries to move away or hide from any attempt to study it. To be effective in this area means the methods and tools used must stop getting in their own way by creating so much extraneous information that an actual threat goes unnoticed, or can hide in the open within all the noise. Much of the difficulty is the result of many products and tools that live in their own data silos and, in essence, are single-purpose systems blind to everything beyond their design capabilities. These may do one specific job well, but they are blind to anything outside of their expertise. This focus in limited areas can impact other systems' abilities to do their job because none of the data each of these systems gathers or uses necessarily feed into an integrated, intelligent investigative environment so the data has shared analysis or are viewed together. This limits many solutions capability to deliver meaningful, dynamic insight into an issue (or issues) such as how a piece of data may be more broadly relevant than just as a single thread from one silo product. Increasing capabilities need to come from improving the extraction and correlation of security, network, and systems information within their data interrelationships to establish meaningful overall network and security intelligence for the entire computing environment. A solution also has to address the industry recommended methodology of layering security systems. This is moving to a point of diminishing returns and is creating the tendency for a security-intelligence-processing black hole based on the mass of data they produce. That black hole comes from different security applications' noise regarding threats, incidents, and alerts from the many layers together inside a network or even on a single device. As a technique most security companies generally endorse and many organizations follow, the point is to deploy multiple applications on a device or within a network so that if one security system misses a threat, the next one may catch it. Layering is deployed within key data resources where there would be, for instance, antivirus/antimalware (AV), *data loss protection* (DLP), firewalls, e-mail security, and other security applications supposedly working together. The results are companies deploying ever more security resources in a layered fashion, yet without a respective increase in shared threat intelligence between them. This further obfuscates organizations ability to determine whether or how well any or all those layers are working as a whole for better security. The drive for layering is at a tipping point of confusion in determining what might be the positive returns from their efforts from using a complex layering methodology. This is making it difficult to answer the question as to whether devices, systems and data are more secure, how secure, or secure at all.

In fact, an expected value return from adding yet more security has diminished due to the ever-increasing price tag of the complexity it continues to introduce, and the resources required maintaining it. Constant changes to systems from updates, new applications, and new users, along with the increased sophistication and volume of threats that need to be dealt with, keep the elephant within the periphery of awareness because these systems can't see more than one part of it. Just adding more systems simply can't address this issue.

To address this requires security-intelligence that has the ability to incorporate all tools' and systems output to maximize visibility and intelligence about the systems, data and threats. This could act as an overseer to turn these raw data outputs from individual solutions and tools into intelligence about the entire environment. It needs to allow a complete view of the elephant, regardless of its current state or position, by enhancing existing solutions' output through intelligent assessment of the data that is output together. This must be done within the context of the entire security environment instead of adding yet more point products with a single narrow view of their output alone.

The adage that it's difficult to know where you need to go unless it's first known where you are couldn't be truer than in security today. The solution is not more security products, but to be able to create a better overall security picture by making more efficient use of what is available today. This would be by enhancing methodologies and systems that can take advantage of the incredible volume of information network and security systems already produce. It's not necessarily a lack of information but a lack of the ability to utilize all that the various systems produce into a cohesive, dynamic and relevant threat picture. We need to use the available systems and extract new knowledge by connecting the dots of all the "elephant's parts," to form a complete picture in a static state with a continuous dynamic outlook into threats the combined data may indicate

It isn't constructive to state that security has failed; that is not the case. At the same time it's crucial to clarify that within its capabilities, implementation styles, overall technology, and methodologies, security is struggling to live up to newer organizational and individual requirements and modern attacks. This is on everyone's shoulders—the industry, organizations, and professionals alike. At the same time, we shouldn't kid ourselves; there is no silver bullet that will allow us all to achieve a completely secure computing nirvana. The truth about protecting data lies, for better or worse, somewhere in between. Wherever that point may be, it has to continually improve over what is being delivered and implemented today. It's up to organizations, and the security industry as a whole, to recognize and admit built-in weaknesses in security systems and network design implementation, operation, and methodologies used in this complex, constantly moving world. Only by accepting the issues can we have a chance to move forward with comprehensive and robust solutions that address the threats as they are today, not ten years ago.

More than anything, I want this book to be thought provoking and bring a different slant to the dialogue about what makes sense in considering approaches for securing data. There are smart people out there who can certainly step in and help guide the direction in which we need to head, with this book simply as a conglomeration of experience, discussions, and consideration of issues and possibilities gathered over the years. There is no time like now to consider what is in front of everyone. It's hoped we can avoid any self-serving aspects from any organization, private or public, but focus to determine what's in the best interest of all organizations, individuals, and society at large.

As a result of this short journey, I hope to have a better picture of the proverbial elephant and how to better see it as it dances its way around and on everyone's data. This also means having thoughtful discussions intended to solve the problems; otherwise, the alternative is we all end up with the unfortunate remnants of the elephant's elemental processes. Understanding that it's critical to quickly identify and manage what is in the room from the start gives us a better chance of utilizing precious time instead of just reacting and cleaning up a mess after it has taken place. It's important that we capture and enhance visibility and intelligence before the lack of either further contaminates our computing systems and data. If we can do the former, we can fully take advantage of the incredibly powerful computing systems to better everyone's lives.

Chapter 1

Computing in the Age of Everything

The new frontier of computing—from the connected car to health and fitness devices and from smart refrigerators to intelligent factory robots—has been predicted in different forms numerous times. This conglomeration of devices and information flow is referred to as the "Internet of Things" (IoT). In 1999, Neil Gross, professor of sociology at the University of British Columbia and a visiting scholar at New York University's Institute for Public Knowledge, said, "In the next century, planet earth will don an electronic skin. It will use the Internet as a scaffold to support and transmit its sensations."

So now there are watches with sensors to monitor an individual's physical state and ship the content off via Bluetooth or some other narrow broadcast methodology to a receiving device. Once received, compilation and analysis can be performed on the data, perhaps with the intention of alerting medical staff of a potential condition, or of an actual emergency, or just to record and analyze physical activity. Information gathered from this device can also be correlated with other information from other devices, displayed on large screens to better enable a viewer to see and analyze it and look for cues from the mix of data. A device may be local in that it only connects within the owner's device family, or it could have global connections and be able to upload or download content to remote systems within the amorphous thing-of-things called "the cloud" (more on that later).

A question that needs to be asked by society, but is already being driven to redefine our world and our view, is whether people and societies either wish to create or augment reality, and if so, what are the benefits of doing so. Clearly all social media and other elements of the ongoing electronic tidal wave have altered reality already, changing how we interact, both inwardly and outwardly. New expectations of our interactions with personal, societal, and world views are already a part of the framework of people's lives today, whether we like it or understand it. In the area of security, all of these new devices and their interfaces represent a multitude of new access points and doors to places that security has no control over. The fact is we need to better capture the flow of information within these systems to better understand their influence on each and every respective arena security is slated to protect.

Regardless of the current hype as to the origination of the "Internet of Things" (IoT), it effectively arrived far before anyone called it by this name or had even considered what connecting ubiquitous devices, or "things," to each other meant. What could be called a "thing" in the 1960s or 1970s to a layperson of that time was a device that could perform a useful task for an expert. For instance, troff[3], which is an old document-processing software system developed by ATT for UNIX, was a programmable input language (document processing = a word processor) that had the ability to have areas designated on a screen for elements, such as fonts, spacing, paragraphs, margins, and footnotes, which is something we've taken for granted for decades now. This is done by today's word processing or publishing applications that everyone uses. A connection that might be made to on old processing system could be an input device, such as card-punch reader (a thing), for loading in a computer program or some type of an output device, such as a printer (another thing), run by troff to produce printed output on a printer of that era. It meant the devices had to have some type of a physical link (or means to communicate between

---

[3] Wikipedia troff

devices) to another type of computing device that all of us take for granted today.

The telegraph, which has been around for well over a century, connected ubiquitous devices (IoT) into a physical communications network, using agreed-upon electrical-pulse patterns or code as the means to communicate information. At the time of the telegraph, the creators, readers, and translators of the pulses were human. As long as a message or some form of information can be transmitted and read between two or more devices or parties, you essentially have a network with "things" attached, crude as one may be when compared to modern systems. If you think about a town of any size in the heyday of the telegraph and a person coming in to either send or get a message, the device that message came in through certainly looked like no other "thing" that person may have been familiar with. So though it wasn't coined as the IoT at the time, it surely was a "Connection of Things" (CoT) that allowed fast and efficient communication relative to its time in history.

The IoT scenario today enables the complete mobility of information regardless of whether it's mundane or high value content. It also means that whatever the value the content may have it lives indefinitely everywhere and nowhere. As well, a content owner may no longer even have knowledge or actual control as to where there content will end up or who may have access to it. And in all likelihood, the content will outlive the actual creator. This is another avenue that continues to exacerbate the risk to information and its owners, whether on a personal level or for an organization. Any area content exists is a potential environment that always has some risk of exposure. For instance, environments that use industrial SCADA (Supervisory Control and Data Acquisition)[4] devices that

---

[4] SCADA is a system that operates with coded signals over communication channels providing the control of remote equipment

communicate within a factory floor, as well as to their company's business systems, could have information related to each device stored all over the place. The SCADA devices can have information that relate to production results, operational parameters of production or other systems, and areas that can impact product quality—all of which might be a target for a competitor or state actor. The factory's computing systems may be monitoring and comparing specifications during product runs while compiling information and delivering reports to other production systems or a management system for data compilation and review.

All the activities of any production system can take place within a single factory or include multiple facilities located anywhere in the world in order to calculate, monitor, and manage important production, material, inventory and other business aspects. The interchange of information between factory systems allows operators to better keep devices functioning within operational guidelines for goods production as well as keep inventory and supplies at levels the organization requires, whether for just-in-time or other types of manufacturing inventory control. And, most likely, production systems, from factory floor systems to their controlling servers can contain specific intellectual property, for instance about a product or a product process that would need to be protected. They could also contain information on production capabilities, potentially costs of production, along with other types of information that an organization will usually want to keep private.

The Connection of Connections for IoET
Modern device interconnections constantly recur, taking place when something is being sent and/or received between systems, making intermittent connections for short durations based on the overall communication specification between various devices and systems. During transfer, devices are not really connected

but are, in essence, doing controlled handoffs of information between multiple devices. I contrast this with a connection that is either a direct physical link or a dedicated path through a network to guarantee the traffic flow and communication process speed between multiple devices. Being able to ensure streaming information operates at a specified minimal rate can be done by logically locking down a portion of a network between devices so that no other device can impact the rate for that communication activity. This is a very useful capability in use today to support areas such as video streaming and other high bandwidth demand technologies.

Today's networks transmit and process information utilizing various units of data. For our purposes here, I'm going to use the term *packets* to refer to any communication between devices. An important point here is that whatever the communication, it happens so quickly and effectively that users don't perceive much in the way of a delay. Any transmission of information passes between communicating parties and through many intermediaries so quickly that, for users, it looks real-time as though on a dedicated link. The communication from a transmitting system doesn't need direct information from a receiving system's physical or network location since intermediary devices can contain all the required information, utilizing an endless selection of paths to deliver the necessary communication requested. The communications taking place today may be from person to person (via some type of viewing system), person to device, device to person, and device to device.

Internet of EveryThing...
From All Devices & People, To All People & Devices...All the Time

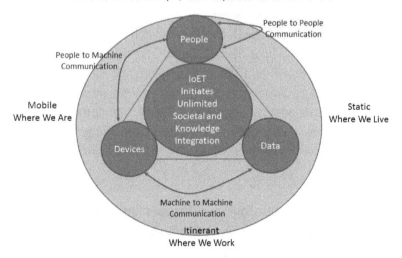

Originally, connectivity between two devices was achieved through hardware systems being physically wired together. Any ability to change connections occurred via a physical relay switch that controlled the link for a circuit between devices through physical wiring. The first instances of this method with a computing device (phone systems worked this way for years) were seen around 1940, when the Complex Number Calculator (CNC) was demonstrated by performing remote calculations on a CNC located in New York while being controlled from Dartmouth College in Hanover, New Hampshire. The link was achieved via a teletype system connected by special phone lines. At that time, I doubt the computer professionals working on this had been considering the massive implications this event foretold. Clearly it would be difficult for anyone to have envisioned how this or any activity leading up to or following it could have created the outcome of today's Internet. A further development in the foundation of connectivity was set in the late 1960s through the advent of ARPANET, which was specified through the efforts of a company working with a US government agency. This subsequently became the standard that the government adopted as the foundation for networking.

The Internet Is Conceived

The earliest ideas of a computer network for general communications among computer users was fashioned by computer scientist J. C. R. Licklider of Bolt, Beranek, and Newman (BBN), in April 1963, as a "Intergalactic Computer Network." From this initial idea, the US government produced the ARPANET specification contract, with BBN as the crucial creator. From that contract, ARPANET was born around 1969. The initial system was designed to support and benefit universities and military communications. Over time, the full benefit of being interconnected became readily apparent and began to quickly spread to other areas. This initial stage of its creation as the "Internet of Things" became the foundational ancestor to its birth. It was only a matter of time before more "things" became suitable devices someone would determine should be able to connect and then access and share information. As we know, as momentum got going, everything became suitable for connectivity.

The Internet as we know it today is, within its global existence, more of a multitendriled, cognitive beast with a dynamically shifting orientation, based on throngs of billions of unseen devices and users. At the same time, the devices and paths utilized are unbeknownst to either its users or the tendrils of the beast itself. It's like an endlessly growing octopus with unlimited arms that continuously wraps around it. Its suckers represent evermore devices and its arms evermore paths. This beast has brought about a new millennium of human existence that is intertwined in an extremely complex and powerful web of computing-oriented and driven human relationships. The computing octopus we call the Internet continually grows as an unknowable, unmeasurable, and, for every person and organization, an unmanageable information ecosystem. Its tendrils offer entrance and exit trajectories in places no one could have envisioned even five years ago, much less seventy years ago at the birthplace of the first connection between the Complex Number Calculator computer and a remote device.

Today, in order to discover all the trajectories and places data passes or is stored and where it's accessed would take time and resources beyond the scope of any tools or systems currently available. Even if those resources or tools existed, by the time the research process could discover the above, the information gathered would be out of date because the computing ecosystem, the Internet, would have changed. Any results are obsolete as soon as they can be observed. In a sense, the Internet is a quantum-world octopus, where any attempted observation impacts the observed such that the observer can't actually determine where something is or how it got there because of the nature of the observed parties continuous changes. It's as though the mere attempt at observation impacts what can actually be observed. A similarity would be looking at a window's reflection of a street out of the corner of your eye and seeing something move, but when you look directly, nothing is there that you had thought you observed in the window. What you thought you saw could be a vagary of the wind, a shadow from a cloud, a moving car's window reflection, or many other things that can't be locked down. Like that fleeting reflection, Internet traffic is in a constant motion that makes it difficult to focus within it. Even if you freeze your position, the observed is never frozen. Various sciences have this same problem. Whether it's quantum mechanics, anthropology, or sociology, all are plagued by the fact that an attempted objective observation of a subject impacts the subject being observed in unquantifiable ways. Strange as it may be, the mere act of observation influences a subject's observable condition. The Internet just happens to be a human-built construct that seems subject to this same whimsy.

There aren't any organizations around the globe able to actually map out every Internet path or device. And if there are, like the

NSA, they likely won't be making any public announcements about any ability to do this anytime soon. Despite how complex even an attempt to do this would be many organizations need to continually map out as much as they can within their own limited operating domain. This is necessary so that they can try to create and apply standardized controls for both internal and external computing environments within their known available systems based on as current a map as possible of their own computing landscape. They need to have as much data as possible as to the number, type, location, users of devices connected to their network. This needs to also include where any data may be going, and where their network may extend when the devices in use are connected to it. Identifying and tracking all this information within their own sphere of computing is, in effect, an endless discovery, monitoring, and management task for any organization.

The intention of any organization in continually assessing their network and its devices is to help ensure availability of the computing resources and data to authorized users. A part of this activity should include making sure transient or stored data isn't put at risk from inappropriate access or unauthorized use. This is an important goal for companies in their continual effort to manage and secure their infrastructure. Ensuring data integrity has been the case whether computing was the primary means of data use and storage or it was originally physical filing. Keeping organizations data safe and accessible for appropriate parties has been a part of centuries-old data-management efforts. The advent of electronic versions of this process has made the practice and protection very different from the past. It has made it both better and worse— stronger if it's all well understood and tight controls can be applied. However, it can be much weaker because the avenues for exposure are so much greater than it ever could have been with physical files. The power to create and store such massive amounts of data introduces yet another conundrum organizations must adjust to and manage—much more data means many more problems simply trying to figure out where any or all of their data may be located or available at any particular time.

Massive and Growing Data

The sheer amount of data generated in a year, along with the accumulation of it over time, puts a lot of stress on every organization and their staff's ability to design and manage logical locations for its use and storage, and to implement effective security protection for the data. To emphasize how difficult this is for everyone, note that a milestone was reached in the early part of the twenty-first century. That milestone occurred when the annual amount of new data created in one year was greater than all the data humanity had created up to that point throughout its prior history. To provide some context as to how large a problem this is, the numbers from one site, Factshunt (see table below) has estimated the amount of data stored on the Internet at the end of 2013[5]. And note this number is, of course, continually growing, with the expectation for robust annual growth to continue for the foreseeable future. Also, for clarity, the term data being used here is an identifiable item of information or content stored on a system that is created by some human action. This is separate to all the data that various systems and applications may create as a part of their operations for things like system management, errors and logs along with thousands of other system activities. For our purposes here, I use the terms "data," "content," and "information" interchangeably throughout the book. Overall, I default to Wikipedia's ample description of the relationship between these various descriptors.

- 14.3 Trillion: Live webpages
- 48 Billion: Webpages indexed by Google Inc.
- 14 Billion: Webpages indexed by Microsoft's Bing

---

[5] http://www.factshunt.com/2014/01/total-number-of-websites-size-of.html

- 672 Exabytes: 672,000,000,000 Gigabytes (GB) of accessible data
- 43,639 Petabytes: Total worldwide Internet traffic in the year 2013
- Over 9,00,000 Servers: Owned by Google, the largest in the world
- Over 1 Yottabyte: Total data stored on the Internet (Includes almost everything)

  Note that a Yottabyte equals 1,000,000,000,000,000,000, 000,000 bytes

Other sources that spoke about the amount of data and all Internet sites pointed to one thing—webpages and the creation of new or modified content is growing and will continue to grow exponentially. As mentioned above, it's impossible to get a final data number because as soon as you do, more data is created and saved. This growth factor can be further represented by considering the amount of continuous growth in processing power necessary to accommodate what I consider to be a "big bang" data explosion. The power to process all this data is hidden behind hundreds of millions, now billions with IoT, of devices that display their content via human-friendly interfaces. In front of these interfaces are users who have no idea, as well as no need to know, the tremendous amount of processing taking place in order to provide them with the information they are currently viewing or listening to. This reinforces the story of the overwhelming amount of growth in data by the massive increase in computing power required to provide a global-systems skeleton that enables processing capacity to support all this data creation, capture, utilization, and storage. Data and computing growth is on a scale never seen before in human history and will likely continue in this manner for the foreseeable future. It is also a socially disruptive activity, changing how people relate, how business gets done, and putting various societies on the verge of growth or collapse. Growth in this area can either accelerate the constructive or destructive aspects of any society. As such, we must use it at our own risk or benefit, understanding that how it's applied can be the ultimate determinant of the value to any society.

The estimate for domain names is anywhere from 750 million to over 1 billion. This number is also constantly changing with approximately 10 percent no longer used and generally left dormant each year, while there is an additional 20 percent or more new sites—a net of up to 75 million new sites a year. The impact of this mass of new and dormant sites represents the complexity of internal and external networks that are creating, supporting, feeding, extracting and storing massive amounts of data. A lot of data can seem to be in almost constant transition. Because of the huge amounts moving as well as stored data, securing all of it is forcing the need for more comprehensive capabilities in order to better address the dynamics of data's nomadic lifecycle.

The Data-Multiplier Effect

Currently, much of the data created by a single individual can get multiplied out hundreds or thousands of times. What may have been a simple original body of content can grow exponentially based on others' access and utilization of it. To put this in perspective, fifty years ago, there just wasn't enough technology available for any single individual to have the content or data he or she created to get multiplied beyond its original form. Today, even trite data is multiplied as technology gives unlimited access to it, thus allowing others to use it to create whole new streams of data. In the past, the content people created were books, articles and writings and letters to each other. These materials were ultimately stored in some form of static system, such as a simple shoe box for the less formal type of data or content, or in file cabinets or storage systems for more formal communication writing.

Today, every human being, via direct or indirect connection, is a part of a global computing skeleton that can create and mobilize masses of content at a moment's notice. This creative system builds upon itself through content exchanges between individuals (known and unknown). As it is exchanged it can easily be reformulated into something new, which speeds the growth of content at an ever faster rate than completely new original content could do alone. This multiplier effect can take a single bit of content, then alter and link it within other points in a digital fabric so that it's stretched, becoming numerous new streams and forms from multiple new creators. At some point, the source of the original content may not even be known. In many ways, it's like that endless rumor that gets added to, changed, reformatted, and retold into a new rumor or story as it's passed between individuals, with the result often totally different from the original in both form and content.

The multiplier effect doesn't mean much if the data may be inaccurate—there is much that is reputable—but it does make it more difficult to tease out the facts from the irrelevant or just plain garbage. The good and the garbage both get constantly repeated within the Internet's forum of expression. This medium allows others to see and resend any content, often unwittingly as to its truth or not. They can also repurpose it into yet more forms—some for honorable purposes, but others unfortunately not. The key is that the individual data explosion means that a person now involved in this process can create more information within the scope of his or her daily life than an individual living a century ago would likely have created over their entire lifetime. There are, of course, exceptions to this, from great authors that span civilizations and generations to great thinkers. However, they were by far the minority in years past. The vast majority of the human race has lived and perished in obscurity.

One hundred years ago, even one thousand years ago, our ancestors unknowingly set the stage for this incredible expansion of information. This is the accumulation of knowledge, gaining wisdom, and building data resources in order to exist, thrive, and better understand the world. Because of the nuances and quirks of humans, we end up with a mix of diamonds and coal all stitched together into a comic mashup of information we call the Internet. There are many stories that describe the conundrum of how to see value from the rubble of information or a situation. What I feel is one of the more elegant and thoughtful depiction of what we're all bequeathed within this area is reflected in the paragraphs below.

There was a brilliant anthropologist, Loren Eiseley[6], who, in his book *The Immense Journey*, wrote a poetic and beautiful parable that describes the constant balancing of conflict we all have to contend with. It goes like this:

> Once upon a time, there was a wise man that used to go to the ocean to do his writing. He had a habit of walking on the beach before he began his work. One day, as he was walking along the shore, he looked down the beach and saw a human figure moving like a dancer. He smiled to himself at the thought of someone who would dance to the day, and so, he walked faster to catch up.
>
> As he got closer, he noticed that the figure was that of a young man, and that what he was doing was not dancing at all. The young man was reaching down to the shore, picking up small objects, and throwing them into the ocean. He came closer still and called out, "Good morning! May I ask what it is that you are doing?" The young man paused, looked up, and replied, "Throwing starfish into the

---

[6] Loren Eiseley. *The Immense Journey*.

ocean." "I must ask, then, why are you throwing starfish into the ocean?" asked the somewhat startled wise man. To this, the young man replied, "The sun is up and the tide is going out. If I don't throw them in, they'll die." Upon hearing this, the wise man commented, "But, young man, do you not realize that there are miles and miles of beach and there are starfish all along every mile? You can't possibly make a difference!" At this, the young man bent down, picked up yet another starfish, and threw it into the ocean. As it met the water, he said, "It made a difference for that one."

As the table on the amount of data for 2013 doesn't indicate, the mass of content can go from high value, even beauty, to the truly ugly. The raw volume of "stuff" those numbers represent is awe-inspiring, as is the effort that has taken place to get to this point in time. As in Eiseley's story, we may want to pick up every piece of content and treat it as though it's all equally precious, unfortunately in the world of the Internet there are many cases where content is not worth any effort. Pertaining to important data, we need to make a difference one step, or one starfish, or piece of crucial data at a time, and ensure we properly protect the content pieces as appropriate to its value.

The need for massive storage along with the number of systems needed for processing creates a level of complexity in computing and security that requires adjusting thinking to address a vast digital environment. It must be considered an ecosystem along the lines of a complex biological entity. Any object or substance needs to be addressed as a part of a whole, not as an isolated entity outside all other computing or individuals and organizations around the globe. As an ecosystem, every part has to be thought of inclusively, which must be true for computing devices, data, and how security is addressed within user communities. Going forward, analysis, design, and architecting systems need to have better means to embrace the entire computing organism, not just one computing element within and organization.

Security, IT and systems professionals obviously require special skills to be capable of doing their jobs. Within the context of designing and maintaining the best possible security protection, these professionals must also be general practitioners in many related areas, with deep understanding of their network, systems and the variety and type of content within their own environment. For better or worse, there is no longer any part of an organization's computing sphere that exists in isolation from any other, or from the outside world. This drives the need for a broad yet deep understanding of their computing sphere not only within its own domain, but how all its computing relates to external parties. Regardless of an organizations desire to stay apart from the rest of the global computing world, the fact is that no organization or individual can any longer remove themselves from global computing, no matter how hard they may desire or try to do so. Simply put, for better or worse, we all are inextricably linked.

Chapter 2

A History of Cybersecurity

Electronic security in the computing environment did not come about at the same time computing systems were developed. It was more of an afterthought, following the foundation of shared computing having already been laid with network protocols, hardware, and system and application software. Initial computing security typically consisted of physical security deployed to protect access to physical systems within their environment. The first expression of computing security was the policies and procedures for accessing systems and data that predate subsequent software security focused on interconnected networks of computers. Security as we think of it today was an offshoot of some of the initial virus attacks. Some smart people realized this was an opportunity around which to build a business, leading to the advent of a number of the original antivirus security firm's decades ago.

The introduction of computer attacks was the first time someone created software in a manner intended to directly compromise other people's systems and data integrity. Initially, these were primarily aimed at publicity for bragging rights, consisting mostly of pranks by college students showing off their programming capabilities. At first, any target was the unlucky computer user who ended up getting the virus code, usually e-mailed or delivered in some form that didn't raise any alarms. In its infancy, often the biggest impact anyone suffered was a bothersome and obnoxious event with inconsequential impact on data. The impact all of us see today from hacking activity is far more lethal and serious to anyone unfortunate enough to be a victim.

The current threat players are far more aggressive, sophisticated, intrusive, and financially capable, whether they are simple criminals or state players. As we all know, unlike past hijinks, the threat actors (hackers) of today have the potential for having a devastating impact on individuals and organizations. To protect against attacks, the antivirus (AV) industry and its basic signature, or pattern-oriented protection, uses a stored database of identifying information about a threat so it can recognize a specific virus, *malware*, or malicious website that may be attached or in the body of an e-mail, and then blocking an identified threat. This system was spawned out of pranks that, over a short time, have grown into evermore destructive activities. As the level of attacks grew, AV grew in capability in response to the continually more frequent and sophisticated efforts of threat actors. The basic antivirus technology most of us are familiar with is the original foundation for an entire industry. Today, that industry has branched out into a large number of companies and security solutions, along with very sophisticated tools to deal with both the old and the continuous flow of new threats.

The result of all this activity in security are thousands of companies that offer vastly different but continuously more complex security solutions to address threats. The majority is designed, in theory, to be combined and thus enable the protection of every aspect of everyone's continually expanding electronic life. A part of this continuous implementation of security has resulted in a huge volume of signature-and-pattern-file type security systems as the basis for a variety of protection capabilities. The volume of security systems, along with constant changes and alterations to systems and policies, continues to complicate successful protection. When you then add new sophisticated hackers who exercise all kinds of old and new tricks and constantly barrage targets in order to open a door, a lot of confusing noise is created beyond what simpler signature and pattern systems are able to deal with. Once in, standard attacker protocol is to disable attending security and make alterations in logs or other areas to mask their entrance, subsequent movement, and any follow-up activities. Once they have successfully inserted themselves into a site, the goal is to maximize the time inside, to identify and quietly extracting the information they came for in the first place.

As has been the case and continues to be now, for better or worse, the security industry has always tended to react to threats, regardless of the level of sophistication or expertise of either the actual threat or hacker. There are parts of industry solutions that has gotten better at "protecting forward" by basically trying to understand and anticipate how a threat or attack process may progress, thus structuring defenses to better protect against these methodologies. A goal within that framework is to identify when one is taking place and act before it can complete its process and create damage. Unfortunately, the reality is that most of the industry hasn't been able to anticipate or plan for a next attack let alone all the differing styles of potential attacks. Though there are definitely some technologies that are designed to better address the changing nature of attacks, it's generally still a game of catch-up. Part of the problem with many solutions is they are committed to a style of defensive technology where changing their products core design can put a company and the products revenue stream at risk. On top of that, to introduce a completely new solution is just not easy or quick as it can require wholesale design changes, years of programming by a company in a new product to address the moving target of modern threats. This is not only difficult but brings with it significant risk to companies existing business models.

And even with a successful discovery of an attack, luck often seems to be on the hacker's side. This is because the time for defenders to sort through all the data in order to recognize an issue and stop the theft of data (*exfiltration*) usually happens well after a threat has already been in process. Though reaction time of systems and the humans using them has improved, the next effort in protection must be far more forward thinking in order to thwart an action before it can be embedded or at least before it has the chance to create damage or take anything of value.

A common perception for many years is the incorrect hope that a good defense can be based on hardening a network edge and all its devices as an effective protection methodology. Even as this approach has been modernized over the years with ever better firewall and other edge based technology designed to keep threats out of a network in the first place, threats have not decreased. Unfortunately, this style of defense has not been able to live up to modern threats for some time. For instance because the edge of a network they're supposed to base their protection on may no longer be identifiable. Every edge device can't be hardened if you don't know what or where they are or who may actually own them. Relying primarily on a hard-shell approach alone is no longer a judicious or effective methodology. This strong-skin philosophy directed not only the placement of security systems, but also the very design of the products. In either case, their placement or design hasn't been able to fully address the need for a flexible environment that allows a significantly more proactive form of security defense, anywhere in a network, not just at the edge. The original hard skin approach has morphed into multiple hard skins through layering of security products on devices within their networks. Regrettably this has been further lulling many organizations into thinking that they had taken care of their security issues. The problem is that neither traditional placement nor the design of these types has provided cohesive network visibility and intelligence capabilities; thus, even with layered defenses, organizations have not been able to stop what they couldn't initially detect or subsequently identify as suspicious activity. The gaps in this approach are much clearer after the many unfortunate incidents that have shown how these defenses can be bypassed. The discovery that an organization's edge was quietly penetrated long ago—that their hard-skin barn had many knotholes and a "*Trojan*" horse could be pulled through them—has driving the realization that a hard skin is only meant to give you time to discover a breach, not stop it. Unfortunately, a discovery was often made after too much time had already passed and damage was already done, generally with the breach caught by an outside party because the damage had become so evident and public.

Security Complexity Stifles Its Capabilities

In 1903, magician and inventor Nevil Maskelyne disrupted John Ambrose Fleming's public demonstration of Guglielmo Marconi's purportedly secure wireless telegraph technology. He basically hijacked the demonstration so he could send insulting Morse-code messages through the auditorium's projector[7], which Fleming was using to demonstrate the Marconi wireless systems capabilities. This was, in effect, the first "electronic" hack. The Maskelyne hijacking of Fleming's demonstration served his own purpose of embarrassing and discrediting Fleming before a public audience, of which he was successful at that time.

Efforts to have secured environments and communication between parties in one form or another have been around for thousands of years. This can include a simple physical method, such as a design that can control an entrance to a castle such as a drawbridge, moat or a Barbican that helps to further fortify a castle entrance. Or, in the case of communication, could be a code method so multiple parties can mask any message between them and protect its content from unwanted eyes. The primary difference today is the speed and complexity of the protection methods involving

---

[7] http://en.wikipedia.org/wiki/Timeline_of_computer_security_hacker_history

communication between parties, and the fact that we're fortifying electronic systems, not stone castles.

The changes in today's security methodologies needs to include the means attackers use against any systems that may be handling large quantities of messages (or content in today's case). Obviously an attacker wants to penetrate a system in order to steal, alter or spoof messages. Their goals could be to create a specific reaction from a target such as initiating a change in their defense posture as that may provide the hacker with intelligence about a targets protection methodologies and capabilities. The example of Maskelyne hacking Fleming's wireless device demonstrates the beginning of the new reality for attack and thus protection in the age of communication that is based on electrical power.

Hijinks and harassment of a more benign nature, whether electronic or otherwise, haven't really changed for as long as humans have interacted with each other. The techniques used as well as the level of sophistication and complexity of an effort to embarrass someone to prove a point have changed a great deal. Methods of gathering or providing intelligence or simply stealing have obviously changed throughout history, particularly in conjunction with the increased sophistication of a society. Many of the past actions taken by people to hack someone have been benign in that no real harm, other than humiliation for the unfortunate target, resulted. Such is the case of Fleming with Marconi's wireless demonstration. Of course, this isn't to say that being humiliated or embarrassed is enjoyable, but that's quite different from other more serious level of damage.

In the area of modern computer hacking, initial efforts were laughable in both their sophistication and intention when compared to today's more complex and well-thought-out actions to find and extract items of value from a target. A modern hacking effort can be a proverbial punch in the gut, as in the Fleming example, or designed to make a broader social statement, such as what Anonymous and other groups like it often attempt to deliver with their target selection and intention of bringing their point to the public. A hacker can use techniques such as a *distributed denial of service* (DDOS) or other non-data stealing actions that have high social visibility by impacting a target's ability to communicate or conduct its business. These are pretty simple attacks, where the assailant assembles enough machines (whether a *botnet* of stolen computing power or otherwise) to flood their target site with enough requests that it is either bogged down, resulting in slower responses, or overwhelmed, resulting in a crash.

This type of attack doesn't necessarily destroy data, but it does impact operations by, for instance, crippling an organization's ability to communicate or serve its audience or customers. This can certainly result in business revenue loss and other consequences. Included in this repertoire is the defacement or redirecting of one website to another, let's say, not-so-friendly site. The redirected site could present the hacker's social commentary about the targeted organization, which is usually not complementary. Redirection could also take users to another site that has malicious code, which could download malware onto the unsuspecting user in order to further present the hackers messages, take over the users system, or simply steal from them. Obviously in the latter case, there is damage done to both the target company as well as their users. Usually the effort of posting a protesting message is quite different than an actual malicious act, though neither is benign to a target. Obviously an attack can come in many forms, with a DDOS leaving a target's internal content essentially intact after an attack is over and the target has gotten back online. However, anyone who tried to connect with the target that was redirected and subsequently hacked certainly may have suffered. In that case, the target organization also suffers from a damaged brand and some form of possible liability, along with the effort that must be made to straighten out the mess with the customer and the targets own site.

There are many categories of security solutions, with various listings on the Web that attempts to identify dozens of different classifications, if not more, of different types of solutions. And, more solutions are constantly being created to address new niche vulnerabilities or perceived opportunities or to fill gaps in a current type of security technology. This includes areas in data protection, data security, AV software, database security, information security, computer security, network security, forensics, analysis, vulnerability scanning, and many other areas. Then there are newer categories in the area of *advanced persistent threat* (APT), threat intelligence, and machine learning, with subsequent new ones added as the growing need for effective protection continues, and professionals try and name them based on what a solution is trying to do. A guestimate is that there are over ten-thousand companies who generate their primary revenue specifically from some form of security product or business. As you break this down into more product or service areas, these companies and solutions represent a wide and growing set of categories with an even wider variety of products or services associated with providing some form of security capability.

And, the thousands of dedicated security companies don't include others that might not be classified as a security company on its own. The non-security companies can include every organization with significant internal security practices as a necessary part of their overall business. These companies utilize internal staff in order to customize and support the security systems they buy, they write custom scripts and policies, and conduct various programming for their security environment. Any mid-sized company and above could fit into this category, which totals tens of thousands of companies in the United States alone. Adding to the multitude of security companies are those companies employing internal security practices, home-grown solutions based on their own or commercial software platforms that significantly increases the security industries size. This means the true number of companies with different levels of involvement in creating different types of security solution, whether for commercial sale or not, is massive. Adding up the total of dedicated security companies and those with sophisticated security-oriented offerings, whether they are offered externally or not, means that the various categories and products within the security ecosystem creates a very complex security environment for organizations and professionals. As well, this makes it even more difficult for the hapless user, who is just trying to do their job and don't have a glimmer of understanding of security. Given all this, one can understand why it's problematic to make security work well consistently, let alone at all. The fact that it works as well as it does is a testament to all the hard work that has been and continues to be done by a whole host of professionals. Unfortunately, the reality is that security today seems to be more of a version 1.0, with a lot of variety in security solutions but not in the depth of what is needed to address the dynamic threats being seen today. Defenses need to be modernized to contend with contemporary threats instead of playing within a continual static losing battle where they try to keep their identification databases (signature and pattern files of threats) up to date against threats. Instead, they need to be able to continuously and proactively monitor and review their capabilities within their network to not only detect a potential threat, but investigate it at any level of detail necessary, determining what it might mean to their security posture, and acting quickly on it. These capabilities need to be foundations organizations utilize to gain visibility into their environment with ongoing development of threat intelligence that allow them to better adapt their defensive posture to real-time current threats.

Knowing there are many issues, there are ways forward. A modern response to threats needs to utilize all the information and capabilities of today's security systems together. There is so much information that is lost because of individual system limitations based on their focus. If this information can be gathered, filtered and correlated with the intent to identify and extract information that may be pointing to another system the information source system can't assess, it could help to add to the threat intelligence regarding the overall environment. This could help make what was normally lost information more applicable to other systems in the shared computing environment. The resulting threat intelligence, like a lit compass in the dark, could help guide security staff in what should be ongoing and active threat assessment based on a flow of intelligence as it may affect any system within their entire environment. It should allow them to validate information across their environment resulting in better insight into relevant network and device activity and a more effective defensive capacity.

So, clearly not all is a lost cause for organizations to protect their data, though it's clear there is a constant struggle going on. The information that flows today from security and other systems about their computing can provide additional intelligence and help to address hackers advantages derived by the volume of security system information defenders have to contend with. Today, security companies provide various means to secure data, networks, and systems, whether directly or through management of network activity, systems, design, and consulting services. The number and variation of available offerings as well as the multitude of security companies make it difficult to be clear on how, where and what type of security should be deployed to do its job. The number, options, and volume of messages and solutions increases the confusion for companies in their ability to assess what they need for security. For our purposes here, I use Wikipedia's definition of security as referred to in the Introduction of Cybersecurity,[8] with a few modifications based on my experience. To put it as simply as possible, the goal of cybersecurity is to protect data, both in transit and at rest. The Wikipedia description indicates security can be comprised in so many different ways; on the billions of devices and device types within their operating system, within hundreds of billions of lines of software application code, or perhaps within hardware itself. This extends the bounds as to what security has to do or can do beyond the simple fact that it's about protecting data anytime and anywhere. It's now such a complex picture, both in how organizations try to do this and all the variations of what they have to work with to accomplish it. To make this process more doable, somehow there needs to be much better orchestration of the information that comes out of security and other systems, and as mentioned before, turn that stream of information into usable threat intelligence.

No reasonable security company wishes to be seen as behind the security technology curve when a new solution type is developed by a competitor. At the same time, these organizations must be careful that they don't cannibalize their own core revenue stream by embracing new technology such that it marginalizes what they currently have to offer to a market. In the situation above, the information a buying organization is trying to sort out can become an assault of messaging that can completely confuse what any type of new solution is actually capable of accomplishing and why they should consider a new solution to replace an older one. With the race for security supremacy, many companies claim they have a "next generation" product—a widely used term that means a system with this designation has capabilities to address some new need or type of threat. Unfortunately, when looking at most of the companies that give a product this designation, it becomes

---

[8] Wikipedia Cybersecurity

sadly clear that this is often no more than a "me too" marketing gimmick that often has little of substance to offer a customer. This type of marketing hype can create more information churn so that security and IT department's product assessment is made more difficult when they're simply trying to make sense of a certain type of technology and what benefits it may provide. It's obviously difficult for everyone, industry and consumers alike, because there are so many messages and so much technology that having a clear picture of any advancement is simply tough for everyone to have clarity around. And this isn't an indictment of the industry; it's moving in so many directions at once that many in the field must also try to make sense of whether certain technology is new and what it may mean for them and their business. Confusion on all parts is not surprising. The purpose here is to take the time to consider the state of security right now—the good and the not so good—and the capabilities it needs to advance in order to deal with the threats we're facing today and will potentially face in the future.

Some telling research conducted by Frost and Sullivan and published in an Oct 3, 2014 report, points out the dilemma of too many systems that are derived from to many unclear choices. The research they conducted discussed one company in the report as their example of what they had generally found to be a normal state of affairs surrounding number of security products deployed. The example company Frost and Sullivan referred to had deployed eighty-five different security tools from forty-five different vendors. It further stated that, "With so many tools and technologies to manage, administration and coordination can become a nightmare, especially for larger organizations." This report was referred to in *Bloomberg Businessweek Magazine*.[9] What they found is what I'm

---

[9] Bloomberg Business Nov 10, 2014 Special Issue article "Cybersecurity's All-Seeing Eye"

attempting to point out here—the massive number of solution options available and the mix of potentially incompatible systems that often result in a mix of security tools that create a lot of extraneous traffic and added complexity within the computing environment that's impacted by their combined use.

Note that this doesn't necessarily assert the need for fewer products or companies that develop and offer viable solutions, though I will discuss the reality that there is a point of diminishing returns from deploying yet more security systems. I'm advocating the fact that for organizations to have the most robust, overall security ecosystem, they need to establish a clear understanding of security's core purpose, understand the decreasing benefits of adding more security or other systems, and then plan their efforts around that view. To avoid just adding more also means that they need to prioritize core areas of security and institute a regimen for best practices in building a security ecosystem for their core data. Perpetuating the continuous layering of solutions has gotten to a point of diminishing returns, and tends to exacerbate the problem, with too many complicated systems watching only their small area of turf. The multitude of systems deployed as discussed in the Frost and Sullivan report shows the results by following the example of a layered pile of point solutions, where each may readily address their specific area of security but didn't necessarily share, or even have the means to communicate with, other security products in the same deployed network. In the process, this array of silo security products can create confusion because of their potentially conflicting alerts and information, along with the overall network's security complexity. Within this kind framework, there is a high likelihood that the array of product introduces and may even mask vulnerabilities, creating blind spots merely as a result of all activities the security systems will generate.

A common theme advocated for many years, as mentioned above, is layering security solutions throughout a computing environment. Part of this is to force an attacker to have to go through multiple defenses before he or she can completely penetrate an organization's key data stores. This also assumes a robust enough capability at each point that a hacker will be detected during this process. There is some value in layering, but the return it can provide can diminish as the addition of one more system can increase complexity to the point where the problems created from the complexity outweigh any incremental benefit from the deployed security system. This technique, taken too far, makes it difficult to determine whether the area in which another layer is deployed to protect can be protected well enough to outweigh any potential negative impact on overall threat visibility. Now that we're all facing the Internet of Things and the potential to add yet more layers, this can simply be another set of points that will exacerbate the complexity layering can introduce. This is because the sheer number of devices and places included in any layering methodology can create so much noise that it can have adverse impact on security ability to manage and protect any, let alone all devices and data.

In spite of the difficult task and attendant complexity, most security company solutions do a reasonable job of protecting what they are designed to protect. Fortunately and unfortunately, the way each product does its job is by focusing on a specific area of interest with products to address the nuances within that particular area. There are a lot of signature or pattern-file types of systems such as antimalware, antivirus software, intrusion detection/intrusion protection (IDS/IPS), and systems that rely on templates, such as data loss prevention (DLP) defined by IT and security staff. A lot of security systems also rely on IT and security-staff constructing access rules, policies and scripts as well as rule engines that all require continuous tuning and adjustment. Any of these techniques can be used by a host of security products such as firewalls, IDS and many other systems. Many of these systems offer a mix of capabilities. These can include multiple unrelated features delivered within a single system such as unified threat management (UTM) or next generation, (NG) with firewall, IDS/IPS, APT, URL filtering, and other capabilities that are supposed to be deployed as an integrated single platform. Most of the features within these systems are normally designed as stand-alone products that tend to have specific operational characteristics that in fact often don't blend well with other systems deployed on the same server or deployed as security services that are supposed to work together. Whether it is UTM or NG, often vendors add these features so they can offer a "suite" to address competitive pressure, to show that they also are leading edge and offer the new technology but in a bundled format so it's easier to purchase. Unfortunately, these don't necessarily provide incremental benefit by being deployed together; it's more a means to simplify product packaging and marketing.

Each security solution may do its job well according to its design specifications, but even those touted as the "Next Generation" security solution do their best work in specific areas. The combined systems, like layering, become its own worst enemy since these systems can do a little in many areas, just not much depth when compared to systems dedicated to specific capabilities. In specific instances combined systems can be a reasonable solution, such as for small sites that can't justify dedicated systems for each needed capability. Even though many of the added capabilities may have value on their own it's not clear that when a primary capability within the product determines the correct place for its deployment in a network a system could also be the correct place for a different capability to work effectively when its running on the same deployed system. Solutions are designed to work in a particular point in a network, whether at the network edge, within it, on servers, endpoints, and deployed as a physical or virtual system. The indicator here is that combining a lot of features on a single system means that system hardware and software likely can't be optimized for any one capability, nor can it be deployed in places optimum for each or any particular feature. This can negatively impact the results of a deployment and create a false sense that a security problem is solved.

All systems any organization deploys connected to the global network are described by most today to operate within "cyberspace," a term coined by William Gibson in a 1982 short story. He later expanded on the concept in the novel *Neuromancer*.[10] Gibson described cyberspace as "a consensual hallucination experienced daily by billions of legitimate operators" and "a graphic representation of data abstracted from the banks of every computer in the human system." Looking at this as it pertains to security, the hallucination is that by continuing to deploy and layer hundreds of individual solutions, with each designed to deal with a specific or individual issue, organizations will be able to protect everything within their computing domain. At the same time, thinking that one combined system can address all the various vagaries of a network and its traffic in a single solution is also spending time in a consensual hallucination. Unfortunately, continuing to think either way is akin to believing that we can all identify every attendee at a large masquerade ball we weren't invited to and weren't provided an attendee list. We can confidently say there were attendees since we could hear the music and may see people streaming in and out. Perhaps we'll be able to tell male from the female (but even that may be a stretch). We may think we can get a gross count, but even that, if people changed costumes before they came and went, would make the task impossible as well. Consequently, we would have no confidence in any of our conclusions as to who came, how many attended, or, for that matter, whether they were all human.

---

[10] Economist Magazine Special Report Cyber-Security July 12, 2014 edition

Today, cyberspace is an environment made up of an uncountable number of devices, of which some unknown number are primarily transport mechanisms to get "information or data" to where we want it to go (routers and switches). Other systems are for processing data (servers, applications, and storage) so it can be in a format and available from a location that users can consume. Many other devices are for local processing and display (desktops, laptops, tablets, phones, and industrial systems) supporting human interactivity by presenting data in an understandable form so that people can use the systems and data for their applied purposes, hopefully to their benefit.

There are billions of complex algorithms built into devices that impact human-to-machine, machine-to-human, and machine-to-machine interactions. These interactions create the Internet of Things (IoT). It's become a hot topic now because past consumer devices were not connected to it until the last decade, but they are now a part of the global computing ecosystem. The buzz today is to connect everything; whether there is an actual benefit or not to doing so for every device is, in my mind, not particularly clear. To many pundits IoT is the predicted result of the global momentum in computing, and the world should embrace every aspect of it. This view is held regardless of what any real or perceived value may be available from any particular device or types of devices to be connected. It seems obvious that there must be some level of human gain or benefit from the connectivity, whether directly or indirectly.

Cyberspace is, of course, hackers' delight. However, it's not so easy for them to ply their trade when you think of all the available targets to sort through; even they have limited time and money, no matter their sponsor. Their advantage is that they can select and then hit an organization constantly until they get in, and the organization has to protect 100 percent effectively against all the attacks they're subjected to. The hacker, however, only needs one success. If you're familiar with Carl von Clausewitz[11] and his writings on war (and these attacks certainly are a form of conflict) he spoke about the inherent superiority of defense and the means required by an attacking force to overwhelm a good defense. Based on the intelligent disposition of defender resources it seemed an attacker needed something like a five-to-one ratio of attacker to defender in order to have a reasonable chance of penetrating a defense. Obviously, based on the strength of an attackers strategy and methodologies, as well as the defenders could change aspects of this ratio. The important point, at whatever ratio it may be, is the defender has a level of inherent advantage that could increase if played correctly or if an attacker played theirs poorly. In the world of cyberspace, it seems that this ratio has been turned on its head, and not to the defender's advantage.

For cyberspace, this ratio seems to be the opposite compared to a conventional physical state of belligerence. Because cyber defenses are static in nature, they make it pretty easy to identify a target as well as their defense posture and the security systems they have deployed. This defender's stasis gives attackers an advantage because they can harness dedicated and potentially unlimited resources, applying a continuous but constantly changing pressure on a defender at multiple points simultaneously and from multiple attack vectors. Then if one considers that any defender will always have a flank or a potential break or weakness in the defensive line, a cyber attacker can continually probe for these for as long as they need as the material cost to them is very low. This alters the dynamics regarding the historic strength of a defender versus an attacker, but not in the defender's favor. In cyberspace, an attacker can organize essentially an endless stream of probes to find a

---

[11] Wikipedia Clausewitz "On War" a treatise on the philosophy and execution of war

defender's flank or weakness, or simply what they use for defense solution. Luckily, one aspect in the defender's favor is there aren't an endless number of good hackers, and they don't have endless resources, specifically time, either. However, when they do focus on a particular target, it's not a matter of whether they will penetrate it, but when, so trouble will brewing for those defenders.

As I'm sure most people have heard this litany, an attacker can fail ninety-nine out of one hundred times in their attempts to penetrate a target; either they were initially blocked from getting in at all or were discovered and removed after they got into a target's system. None of that matters to the attacker because persistence means they're very likely to get in undetected at some point, and remain undiscovered long enough to conduct their work. Once in, it's crucial to avoid discovery, which means they have to exhibit added sophistication in the skills and methodologies beyond the initial penetration of a target system. The aspect of being attacked is like the story of the two people running from a bear, where one stops to put on his or her running shoes so he or she can outrun, not the bear, but the other person. In the short term, being able to run faster (or defend better) than others is a reasonable tactic against attack as long as you have an endless array of others you can outrun. This can, for a while, provide a semblance of safety. The problem is that once the bear has devoured the slower runners, it can now pay attention to the faster runner, which, in this metaphor, may be marginally better-protected organization or simply one that had run under a hacker's radar. In a sense, the running-shoe metaphor illustrates that if one organization is a bit more adroit than another, it may help them to reduce their risk profile for a while. But the fact is that everyone's time will come, whether directly or inadvertently as the bear will always get hungry again, even after a big meal. No one can prescribe when that may be, it may have already happened and the victim company just hasn't realized the bear was already in their midst.

If you're like me and not the fastest runner (not even close) taking the time to employ a short-term tactic, outside of an overall strategy, will likely not buy enough time to warrant the exercise in the first place; however, it may make me feel like I have a better chance, at least for a short while. Since we're all connected, and we won't be less connected in the future, it's time to look at how to build a strategy for everyone's safe utilization of cyberspace. A strategy of hoping I can outrun everyone else—staying far enough ahead to be safe—seems like a fantasy-induced dreamscape that obviously won't hold up. Creating a strategy based on group protection, much like getting vaccinated for a disease so that one benefits from the vaccination of all (or close to all) versus today's individual organization attempting to defend itself needs to be a strategy addressed so we can all move forward.

It Started at the Endpoint

The initial beginning of what most people think of today as cybersecurity started when antivirus software was created to protect users against damage to user desktops by new hobby hackers. Originally, it was made to protect against rogue individuals who were often bent on proving to their peers, or whomever, their superior programming skills. It was inevitable once others recognized that they could get into other people's systems that it would be turned into the very lucrative industry that exists today. The simple fact is that there have always been thieves among us; the question is always based on the current aspects of a society and what tools a thief would use to conduct their thievery. Today, obviously, a high level of sophisticated theft activity is now in the computing sphere.

To start out, my view of *endpoints* is that they are a place where data can be stored, accessed, or manipulated. With this broad of a definition, it can define just about any computing environment in a network. And this is different from "user" endpoints, which are devices dedicated to a specific person or group (such as a public or private web application) for their access so they can create, manipulate and store data. This is the primary area of discussion as they represent the largest and most prevalent attack surface. For endpoints, there is a level of noise in security and industry that traditional user-endpoint protection is dead, that it's not kept up in protection against modern threats and fundamentally not as effective as it once was. There are many instances that do seem to indicate that the effectiveness of security specifically designed for endpoints is having a near-death experience. At the same time, it also seems the need to protect endpoints, if anything, has increased based on the number and success of attacks that originate at endpoints . Does this mean current technology should be thrown away or that it no longer has any value? In my view, the answer to that is a resounding no. Static endpoint defenses may not have the capacity to address a lot of today's more sophisticated threats, but at the same time, if it's removed, then hackers will no longer need to use sophisticated attacks as endpoint entry will be much easier. Every endpoint would be naked to simple traditional attacks which would invite an endpoint slaughter. It seems more that endpoint security needs to enhance the current capabilities of traditional endpoint technologies to successfully deal with modern threats. Of course, this gets back to the issue of adding yet another layer of defense, and thus a potential for greater complexity and processing overhead at endpoints.

To deal with any changes in order to address modern threats, making adjustments in our thinking and methodologies ought to be considered. The resolution to the vulnerability of endpoints must be addressed with a combination of capabilities. This needs to include some means of applying the knowledge of existing threats that traditional endpoint protection (EPP) represents along with a means for endpoint detection and response (EDR) and intelligence (EDRI) to deal with more innocuous and malignant modern threats. To make this work it needs to be an infrastructure that creates intelligence out of data and shares the intelligence within an integrated solution. Until then, layering will have to work. Otherwise, what we're all hoping is for hackers to call a truce on their activities, and leave everyone alone until we can get all the complex security issues figured out. For the time being during their sojourn, perhaps the hackers could spend their time stealing from each other within their own dark industry.

As mentioned earlier, endpoints are the devices where data is either at rest or it's actively being accessed and manipulated by a user. A user endpoint is the device that provides those users specific access to any type endpoint—the one in their hand or servers with their data. No matter the endpoint, users are always the weakest link in protection, regardless of their level of education, expertise, or their intentions. This requires security to constantly monitor users, devices, and data in order to have any chance to protect the data itself. As the proliferation of user endpoint devices has exploded over the last ten years, along with the addition of the Internet of Everything (IoET) devices, the difficulty of protecting any endpoint is becoming a very steep slope. Along with this expanding endpoint world, it seems a lot of thinking reflects the attitude that as a type of technology, endpoints aren't glamorous. As such, security technology is talked about in areas seen as more dazzling to secure, such as virtual systems and the cloud. In fact, based on the definition used here, these are also endpoints, so in many ways, security has been ignoring a keystone concept that asks a simple question as to where it should be employing its protection: where the exposure is, at the endpoint. That's because the externally visible device is the user endpoint as it is the front line.

Whether virtual or cloud systems are endpoints or not, or whether they are getting attention when addressing security products each of these creates unique issues in being able to secure data running within or through them. For instance, in a virtual system, the existence of multitenancy, where organizations and users share processing, storage, and the network brings in many question about who a user may inadvertently be partnering with on a shared server. Clear and absolute separation between all organizations on a multitenant system can be an issue. With virtualization within a cloud, a client's processing and stored data is frequently shuttled between systems based on the business and performance requirements a cloud vendor has for its own operations. In this scenario, trying to keep everything secure imposes additional issues organizations struggle with. It is the case cloud vendors clearly wish to protect their customer data integrity, at the same time this can conflict with their need to provide quick, easy and reliable access for customers. The reliable and fast access customers demand limit the kind of depth of overall security cloud vendors can apply across the board, often leaving more rigorous security choices and added cost up to individual customers. The ongoing problem of rigorously protecting data within an environment of a multitude of different systems' design, a focus on continuous computing flexibility and availability to customers impacts the depth and how security can be implemented. Along with the location, geography or server within a data center running an application in conjunction with the dynamic location of any stored data continually pressures the ability to provide robust protection.

Regardless of the type of computing moniker (cloud, virtual, BYOD, etc.) that may be attached to a computing resource, a principal focus ought to be where the entry point to any data is found. Frankly, it may not be exciting, but the fact is that critical data either ends up spending time on some type of user endpoint, or passes through multiple user endpoints during its processing as a core destination during its lifecycle as well as with linkage to either local or remote storage. It's also true that hackers spend their time working at gaining entry through user endpoints, whatever type they may be. Once in, they then find other internal endpoints where their target information spends time either being processed by user endpoints or stored, waiting for commands related to user requirements for any subsequent processing or movement. Even in the case of backup systems, they are attached to user endpoint devices so share their attack surface. If you look at what Ransomware tries to do, capture and control data, including access of the actual backed up data, in a sense indicates the reality that pretty much everything is accessible via a user endpoint, making them a key priority for protection.

Agents for Security and Monitoring

Throughout security-industry history, a common method of implementing security was to first deploy a software application on a device needing protection. As the number and size of security applications increased, they morphed into using agents on devices that communicated with a core application running on a server. This was clearly more efficient on both processing overhead and storage on any endpoint. Simply defined, an agent is basically a local software application that is a subset of a larger central application. It communicates with the central application to keep it up to date as well as keep the central application informed of its state and operation on an endpoint. This could include locally processing necessary security information on the agents host system. Agents are generally a more efficient means to get a feature on a device where you attain the benefit of its capabilities without the computing overhead a native, full-blown application may require. With links to a centralized security or management system, they can provide local protection as well as monitoring capabilities, and be continually updated as required from the host application. Agents can operate on physical or virtual systems and can be the primary means of securing a device; they can also offer supplementary security for an application considered to be of high value on top of the normal security deployed on a per-device or application basis.

Agents have been a normal element of security and network-management systems for decades. They address many needs, including monitoring devices and applications, and sending resulting information for assessment and correlation of the system an agent is deployed on. Different types of software agents can reside on an individual user device, endpoints, within an application, gateways, or anywhere within a network environment. They can be deployed in such a way as to update a centralized site, providing threat reports or other types of information for analysis and potential action that can be taken according to established security or IT rules and policies. Centralized systems tend to update agents based on established schedules and may be able to correlate information from individual or groups of agents. The comparison of information from multiple agents or systems may help create some basis for determining device activity or threat state with potential recommendations to the system's human manager or automated actions. Those actions can include alerting on or blocking a perceived threat based on an existing policy that are set up within an agent or its management system.

Many more *BYOD* (Bring Your Own Device) devices are being utilized, driving the need to deploy agents on them so they can be securely incorporated into an existing network environment. For better or worse, organizations often have to put multiple agents on devices to ensure that each is incorporated into their overall security and management environment. This means that multiple agents and software components are likely running on each device at the same time. For instance, this could be a separate agent for antivirus/malware, DLP (data loss prevention), encryption, logging, as well as other types of security and systems management. Without careful planning and testing, a greater number of agents can potentially overwhelm a device and management environment as well as increase complexity and the potential for conflict. Also, though there may be a security agent installed on an endpoint, if that endpoint is under attack, one technique used by hackers is to turn any security agent or application off so that it can no longer provide protection or even update a central system. To address this issue, there are different implementations to improve agent's self-protection along with designs to keep an agent from being discovered by an attacker and turned off, thus better safeguarding operational security. If this can be done, it can improve a device's ability to defend itself, essentially giving it the capacity to self-protect, which is an ability that is becoming more critical every year. Ideally, a modern agent makes existing security better by extending its abilities and delivering capabilities to defend against modern threats. Any additional agent needs to add significant value with minimal impact in order to justify adding yet another to an already overly complicated security environment.

Agents and specialized applications aren't necessarily a problem as individual elements within a system; it's the potential number and added complexity they may bring to an already complex area. Some companies have tried to solve this problem by having what they call agentless solutions, which is not quite what it sounds like, as there has to be something resident on a device to be able to monitor it, even if it is not spoken of as an agent. Either it's on the device, or it continually queries devices it's monitoring, which leaves monitoring time gaps as well as can flood a network with yet more extraneous traffic. Perhaps the intention is to imply that the agentless solution is not running on the device but is only reactive to requests; consequently, it only takes resources when requests are made. Perhaps that is true, but as it's a software component, that term is a bit disingenuous to the facts. For gathering information as well as being able to monitor and react, the best place to do that is on a device itself, whether as an active agent or passive respondent code. Either way, agent or agentless solutions still need to link into their application to do their work, again increasing the potential for a more complex environment that still needs to be managed.

Is Endpoint Protection Dead?

As endpoints aren't going away any time soon, the necessity to protect them and the information they process and possess is greater than ever. However, because traditional endpoint protection struggles to keep up with either threat volume or increased sophistication of threats, something has to change. As mentioned earlier, user endpoints are the specific avenue that any threat will come through as well as be the first place an initial threat begins any execution, whether an exploit, spear phishing or otherwise. Once a hacker is past the endpoint undiscovered they can conduct initial scans to determine where to move around in an environment or to a specific internal target.

Since endpoints are the key devices accessed by users who are generally just using a device to do a job, and can't be expected to be security experts, they're vulnerable and need to be protected from their own mistakes. Frankly, expecting the vast majority of users to conduct their activities like security experts, no matter how much everyone thinks they should be security aware, hasn't worked out overly well. Like all of us, they're pressed to get their jobs done using computing devices and applications as tools their organizations provide for these jobs. Because the vast majority of users can never be experts in computing, they will be targeted because hackers understand this reality and take advantage of the fact that the weakest point is always the human on an endpoint.

To address the weakness in human computing interactions, in effect, means humans need to be taken out of the equation all together as a potential threat target. It really isn't possible to continually keep every individual trained to a level of awareness and expertise so that they can avoid inadvertent security breaches. Obviously, users simply can't stop using computing systems, so the only way to eliminate humans as an exposure risk is to design security and user systems that don't allow human users to be exposed. With the growth in the number of users and devices per user, training and education can only deal with the issues at the surface, not at the depth required to reduce the most vulnerable attack surface, people.

Various predictions from a number of different analyst firms put the number of endpoint devices connected to the Internet (IoT) to be over 50 billion by 2020. Whether this number is correct or not, it's clear that the number is going to be exponentially greater than what is deployed today. What may comprise endpoints will be all over the map, including smart devices with minimal human interaction to ones that attempt to assist humans as individual or groups of devices to create a smart home system. As these devices will be connected to the Internet, regardless of what they do or how they are accessed, this will add to the overall traffic and the difficulty of sorting out, simply, what the hell is going on with any single or set of devices? There doesn't seem to be a final number to this volume, so the question of how to reduce or eliminate exposure is a tough ask. We need to recognize that the number, variety, and complexity of the endpoint environment along with the level of skill of most endpoint users are the Achilles' heel in any security profile. As mentioned earlier, this must be addressed effectively to provide the protection needed. When one thinks about the capacity and intention of many of these devices such as a refrigerator or power meter, it's debatable as to the value of having direct protection on them at all. It may be that overall systems monitoring and protection, along with reactive capabilities may be the best scenario.

As mentioned, hackers use social engineering to penetrate targets. This makes device and security design even more critical to ensure that they fit user work styles to inherently secure against mistaken actions. Security needs to be an invisible footprint within the design of any device and application as it may be the only way to ensure user compliance to safe computing. It's been shown that forcing stronger security protection on each device or user imposes enough of a burden that users will try and figure out ways around it, so it's not the best choice. Perhaps device security-layer invisibility with connections to monitoring and response capabilities may be more efficient and fit within most users' social frameworks. This can also be more constructive and remove any pushback from users than trying to apply intrusive and heavy-handed security on them.

Socially Engineering Endpoint Protection

Social engineering for hacking works because it relies on common knowledge and attention gaps humans have in many areas including security as well as to take advantage of users characteristics.

Most computing users know little more about computing systems or their vulnerabilities than necessary to use a system; it's a tool to use along with a couple of applications to do their job. People focus on task completion within the computing tools to accomplish the tasks. If what users see is familiar—that is, if something takes place that fits "good enough" within their current activity—their suspicion won't be raised enough for them to pause in the task at hand. As one would expect, we aren't going to find much reflection by them on whether there is an issue or not based on what they see. The rule in most user-computing activities is to quickly look, click, and go.

If something doesn't raise their suspicion, which is what social engineering attempts to do, users will continue as though everything within the current working environment belongs there. As most threats take time and aren't particularly visible to anyone, noting them would require a mental pause and stringing together a time span of likely innocuous events in order to note that anything may be suspect. This is obviously difficult, as any user has to in essence step out of their current activity and review what may been taking place in their current computing realm that seems odd.

Expecting busy people with interrupt-driven lives to spend cycles noting, let alone investigating, something that a security person may regard as suspicious is a false hope. All the varying types of systems mean users have to be protected within the context of their social and work environments. To expect that they will stop their activities for any moment to do a validity check on everything that passes their way just isn't a reasonable view of how humans go about their daily business. The fact is that if it looks good enough, it's generally accepted to be good enough for most people to simply continue working. However, the most discerning or expert eye in an area along with security experts can, and have, been fooled by a good-enough hacker's social engineering activity.

Endpoint security in particular must be socially engineered to protect users from potentially poor choices and to do so transparently to both the user and hackers. That means a new generation of endpoint security that can both mask users from wrong choices and, when necessary, protect them and their computing environment from exposure to hacker attempts. Social engineering for protection also means the system must have more overall intelligence as to what is taking place within the entire computing ecosystem and user actions as well. It also needs to have the ability for both security and IT professionals to dynamically drill down into events and gather intelligence that enables them to control any activity or potential threat as it takes place.

The capabilities and richness of the World Wide Web when it went from 1.0 to 2.0, delivered a level of increased sophistication available for users in their experience of the Web, and developers in their creative options. Developing new and more powerful software systems that create incredible but secure experience for users and data is where security needs to go today. Currently, a lot of security is still at version 1.0, with the unrealistic expectation that users are part of the protection scheme by being knowledgeable participants. This isn't to say to say users should be ignorant, but it is recognition that a user oriented participation model isn't effective enough. With the success of spear phishing and other sophisticated attack methods such as exploits, this is proving to be more of a falsehood every year. Endpoint security needs to work, regardless of active participation of any normal user. It can do this by first developing capabilities as mentioned earlier in order to protect a user from their own mistakes. It can also extend network threat intelligence and analytics with endpoints in a two way flow without requiring that any endpoint user be actively involved. This is a start to building the foundation for security 2.0—a threat intelligent environment that delivers power to those who have the job to protect data and systems as well as keeping users from making the common mistakes that put data and systems at risk. To complete this and get to security 2.0, endpoints need to be an inclusive part of an overall security ecosystem, and users as participants without them having to know all the details of their participation. The industry is on its way to this, but there is still much work to do to get there.

Chapter 3

Technology-Driven Security

In our technical society, every industry has the same problem: there aren't enough skilled professionals to fill the many complex jobs that are available. In security, this problem is even more severe as the pressure of security and network complexity, along with evolving hacker skills and tools, continues to increase, while the number of available professional staff is unable to grow as fast. With security, the knowledge baseline required for a professional to create and maintain an effective defense also continues to increase. At the same time security professionals have trouble keeping up with current requirements, let alone all the new technologies. Security professionals must constantly enhance their capabilities to not only address more competent hackers, but also to try and keep abreast of the deluge of new products and features. The persistent churn of new features and product means security professionals generally specialize in fewer and fewer products and areas. Realistically, there are just too many systems and variations for anyone to hope to be expert on more than a single one let alone a variety of different systems. The volume of knowledge required is a constant issue for many technical specialties, including areas such as medicine and others that have the need for professionals to possess deep knowledge in particular areas. For better or worse, having deep specific knowledge often means limited knowledge in related parts of the same field. What I consider to be a simple truth is that the continuous application of more technology to address technological issues is a Faustian bargain. If any new technology can't enhance individual or group visibility into their systems to gain greater understanding and clarity for better decision making, then we've just traded one set of blinders for another, albeit perhaps a more colorful set.

Most organizations utilize security industry recommendations for implementation methodologies, such as layering security solutions like a series of onion skins across an entire network environment. This recommended methodology has provided benefits in the short term, but has become unwieldy due to two factors. One is that the attendant systems create so much data that they tend to overwhelm anyone's ability to garner meaning from it. The second is the inability for anyone or any overall system to keep up with the thousands of security solutions, along with the fact that they are all designed to address different areas of a network as well as its applications and data. The continued increase in more products, as well as their variations and options, means that though layering in a limited form makes sense for specific areas; all the various security layers employed today have created gaps. And often the weakness layering can create within security system isn't found out about until a system or the network has been hacked or, if an organization is lucky, during penetration testing. It brings to mind an adage that is common in the security industry. There are two kinds of companies that have been hacked: those that know they've been hacked and those that don't yet know. Today's problem is that the tools are actually making it more difficult for those who have been hacked to know whether and how they've been compromised. Once the compromise is discovered, it's also hard to determine how it happened, what the hackers were after, where they went, how they got in, and what may have ultimately been lost by the organization. Unfortunately, the visibility needed for a company's security staff to quickly and confidently figure out what transpired either hasn't been available or wasn't very usable for most organizations staff, though that is starting to change.

The security industry expends tremendous marketing resources to create unique messaging regarding their ability in threat discovery and protection. Most of the messaging by most companies is about how they can distinctively, in comparison to every other security company, address a particular security problem. The issue isn't whether any of the solutions provide value. It's that each one represents one of many security roadways to an already overcrowded security intersection. The promise of security information nirvana isn't feasible because there isn't a security or network cop to direct all of the security traffic on this roadway. When you include the limited interactions and conflicting information between many systems makes it even more difficult for a security person to gain meaningful intelligence from all the data flows. And, without intelligence, it becomes problematic for them to draw conclusions and deal with a specific incident as well as plan on how to improve protection of their systems and data.

There are various security flows of data pulsating throughout every network environment. These flows often apply limited or minimal means at centralization or intelligence collection from the data, either for better management or to be able to glean insights out of all the data's relentless streams. Ironically, because of a lot of security companies' competitive branding and messaging needs, there generally isn't much, if any agreement on the conditions of a common information roadway or methodologies for reviewing the relevancy of all of data spewed out. A continuous problem is that there really isn't an information intelligent conductor that can make sense out of all their disparate traffic flows such that it can become usable intelligence. This means that security practitioners are constantly allotted partial information about their security state. Obviously only having partial information can make their jobs a sometimes joyless and certainly tougher task in protecting their user organizations and data.

While all security companies can protect various aspects of company networks and data, the lack of a consistent definition for what they are all trying to do at a functional level together, without a deep level of cooperation between systems, means that organizations deploy a lot of varied security solutions that don't work together. Unfortunately organizations often can't expect to have an information flow from their security applications combined or integrated between the applications even when they're from the same company.

What this means is that economies of scale aren't a very effective model for deploying security. That is because deploying more security has to assume each respective new tool deployed will deliver more value than the marginal cost of its specific deployment. That is no longer the case when deploying more security or other tools within a network environment. Even if companies have a similar design and result objectives, a customer is challenged to get consistent or common intelligence to draw consistent and reliable conclusions from even similar systems regarding current threats. This is even more difficult when considering unknown threats which are the more prevalent threats today. The security staff continually wrestle with whether there is a threat right now, what the threat may be, where might it be located and where it may have come from and what is it after. Obtaining this kind of information allows staff to better assess any potential impact as well as any action they should take to address the threat in both the immediate and the long-term.

The differences between security systems and methodologies often means it's difficult to agree on what exactly is or isn't considered a critical event, or even determining whether something critical happened or not. Trying to decide this on a case-by-case basis is a very time-consuming exercise at best for any organization. The fact that organizations often don't have the resources, let alone the systems, to do this makes deriving a useful conclusion from existing information a hit or miss scheme. Doing an assessment as to whether a response requires further investigation is always difficult. Trying to do this through the many layers of solutions and potential combinations of actions causes confusion and creates conflicting information, with the ultimate result being weaker overall security.

Of great help would be some way of normalizing the information coming from all the security systems through common threat classification and unified security systems intelligence. There is some agreement in this area, but unfortunately, the definitions on many players' parts on what these should comprise are reluctantly used unless they provide them with a competitive advantage. Unfortunately, ensuring that there is a rigorous common system is still not as close to realization as it could be. Organizations that implement a variety of security systems, even from a single company, often need to build the relationships between the various systems themselves. And they have to do this against the constraints of staff size, ongoing threats, and complexity of the solutions and their own environment. The intricacy of company computing environments further obfuscates their day-to-day task of protecting data, often putting staff in the position where they have to try to sort out everything going on in their network to identify something of importance. This sometimes seems like forcing a staff to try and count the rivets on a Saturn rocket as its being launched into space from a spot twenty miles away, and all without binoculars.

With the need to monitor the volume of traffic, some means of automating diverse security information processing as well as correlating and flagging information into prioritized categories for more detailed human review and action is the only possible way to keep up. There are small pieces of this now, but a complete system needs enough intelligence to be able to assess and make sense of volumes of abstract security, general systems, and network activity information. This should be done within the context of "big data" analysis to compare, link, assess, analyze, classify, and prioritize the bodies of information coming from all these systems into a level of actionable intelligence for security staff. Then professionals accessing the body of information need to have the tools to further investigate and analyze the intelligence as it pertains to endpoints, servers, devices applications, and traffic on their network in real time as it may relate to any threat, or suspicious activities. With the resulting intelligence from this process, an analyst can more easily and quickly determine when it is appropriate to investigate further into a current suspicious activity. And, when investigating they can utilize forensic capabilities to gain insight and a better understanding of any incidents. This could also be used to actively hunt for any items, files, executables, or others they deem as possible issue indicators, using the results to then adjust their security protection to address all the flagged activities.

The future of a successful security ecosystem requires utilization of many technologies such as a form of machine learning that can enhance human-oriented capabilities. For instance, this could mean simply comparing current traffic or events against known and unknown past and current activities from specific systems, devices or users with the intention of helping to guide and improve human expertise by reducing extraneous information. A goal could be the delivery of a more dynamic forensic analysis that can extrapolate security intelligence in real time so that clearly relevant as well as orphaned security systems data isn't lost. When an event considered to be of little importance can somehow be linked against another seemingly innocuous event, where together they clearly call for further investigation and analysis of a potentially critical issue, then data is being turned into intelligence. The result may be that an obtuse connection between two events could point to hidden threats or an actual hack or exploit taking place that a single system can't spot. Not because the existing security systems can't do their jobs, but because individual systems, by design, generally look at data specific to their area of focus, not an entire computing environment.

Most systems protect specific devices or applications and aren't designed to consider how an activity they detected may pertain to some other device. This means an alert won't be triggered regarding a device they monitor regardless of the events relevance to a different device or application. Security systems on the whole don't correlate what they see as individual events if it may be associated to a particular device or application outside of their purview. An action of this sort would be beneficial since upon further investigation and cross referencing, the data may be determined as a threat to another system. One product's insignificant data may be another's useful data. But two bits of seemingly useless data from two different systems can be a very important bit of intelligence when they are viewed from an associative point of view between systems and data. Unfortunately, more raw information isn't necessarily more valuable, as it can also obfuscate relevant threats and create a shield inside the volume of information flow as a part of network activity. Systems that work within their own silos, as well as they may do the job they're designed for, ignore or lose tremendous amounts of relevant information that may have relevant indicators and pointers to threats inside of the overall network.

An example of how much information a wide variety of systems can create—even when as well structured as possible around product capabilities and staff and business needs—is a retail chain store with about 2200 sites. Each store has anywhere from fifty to one hundred point-of-sale-type (POS) devices connected to local and remote corporate systems. Most of these devices are essentially stationary, but quite a few are mobile for the purpose of tracking store and warehouse stock and inventory status information. Stationary ones are used to accept and process customer card transactions. In this particular case, the count for POS type devices is over 23,000 of these devices scattered throughout their network, generally connected around the clock. And, with POS-type systems, it's not unusual for these devices to have long deployment lives. These systems are often reliant on older proven hardware technology along with older versions of specialized software operating systems and applications. Additionally, when they are purchased companies tend to buy a volume of these devices at once that allows them to deploy the same system across all their stores, easing deployment and maintenance costs. They also try to keep costs down per unit by specifying the minimum required level of memory and processing power for devices to do their jobs. All of these factors within the specifications for a single purpose specialty system make it more difficult to replace, upgrade, or add security capabilities on them at their original deployment or at a later time.

A similar set of parameters to specialized and limited device capabilities is single purpose designed medical equipment. A significant difference with medical types of devices is the additional limitation that a possible change, adding a fix for a security issue or any kind of update to them may require FDA approval for the manufacturer to implement and release the changes. This can notably increase the time frame, cost and complexity for any fix. It may even mean a device in question won't get a fix or patch at all because the time frame and effort to get it done and get approval is thought to be more effort than the value of the fix. It's often better to just come out with a new device and completely replace the old one. Even if a new device is made available, it's often the case an old device will still continue to be used. There are many reasons for their continued use, such as staff and other resources to make a change and purchase cost for a company to replace older devices that are working and paid for.

Trying to update or change any of these types of systems, whether POS or medical devices, can be very time consuming, with the potential for significant impact on day-to-day operations. In POS, the number and built in processing limitations of the systems themselves create issues. With medical equipment, the addition of any risk to patients, as well as regulatory requirements, increases an organization's financial exposure and takes much longer than the benefit of a fix may provide. Obviously all of these can impact both the using organization and manufacturers' ability to keep equipment up to date and current in a variety of areas including devices security capabilities.

There are real consequences with older OS platforms and software versions that can't run the latest security or have no security running natively on them. Any of these limitations don't eliminate the need for some form of security or monitoring of any of these types of device. The exposure to POS systems was laid out in a midyear 2014 Cisco Cybersecurity Report.[12] It stated that POS systems are being increasingly targeted because they're connected to the Internet via a corporate network. This provides criminals with a fairly easy point of entry to an organization's network. Additional complexity comes from the fact that many companies that utilize POS systems within their business use third-party vendors for all or part of their POS solutions. This can provide additional access points for criminals via these vendors' connections. Whatever access point happens to be used as the avenue for penetration, vulnerabilities increase as the number of points to monitor and protect grows. POS and other similar types of systems are a clear example of the problems that continue to plague organizations to provide at least a baseline level of protection for these devices.

Consumer transaction systems like POS communicate with various servers and applications to do their jobs. Those sites accumulate and digest the supplied data, consolidating and analyzing it. They

---

[12] Cisco 2014 Midyear Security Report

also transfer relevant elements to a centralized or other corporate server application as well as bank and credit card systems for authorization and payment. These all require active, 24/7 communications with financial and other institutions to transact business. Behind any processing there needs to be a lot of storage for data. This data can also be accessed for marketing activities that utilize portions of the data as well as other operational aspects of a business's daily activities. With the volume of data, another aspect is this data lives a long time and has many associated places it may be processed and stored, providing many unknown access paths to it. And the longer it exists, stored in an expanding number of places continually broadens its exposure. Whether POS has intermittent or constant connection to a site via multiple networks and subnets, every connected system and storage site needs security in place that effectively provides protection for POS device data flow.

Digitizing Security intelligence

In an article published in *Foreign Affairs* magazine that discussed labor and capital, the authors pointed out a historical maxim; that is, in a free market, the biggest premiums go to the scarcest inputs needed for production. In this context, I'm classifying the specifics of the two categories by putting IT and security staff in for labor (IT) and outlining an all-encompassing databank of threat knowledge (TK) assembled from multiple security data flows along with the tools to apply that knowledge as capital. The articles author says that "as more capital (TK) is added cheaply at the margin, the value of existing (old) capital will actually be driven down." I call it old capital because it's without the threat knowledge (TK) capabilities spoken of here. What this means is the application of TK capital must be a driver to enhance the existing skill levels of labor (IT). The issue surrounding the limited availability of qualified security staff means that to get them to be more productive can only be done by having access to better knowledge (TK) with advanced tool sets so they can apply the knowledge to act on threats faster and more efficiently. This should be a result of more targeted security threat intelligence instead of just incidents or alerts that IT has to spend time chasing down to only find out they weren't a threat. By eliminating incidents or alerts that upon investigating didn't warrant the time to investigate would allow IT to focus on critical areas for investigation and response. The enhancement of labor in this case can be derived from many areas. This can include better filtering of nonthreats from actual threats, more concise information for analysis of any suspicious activity and the ability to quickly conduct focused investigation of threats that have been judiciously prioritized.

To enhance this process, there needs to be deeper cohesion in data sharing between security systems. The alternative is continuing to observe fragments of issues that are more superficial because the system gathering data can't assess what it may mean from one system to another. With the advanced threats of today, this is no longer good enough. Having a system that can gather a lot of the information, such as Security Information and Event Management[13] software (SIEM), is a step in the right direction. These still don't provide any knowledge as they generally can't derive any threat intelligence from the information they gather from systems logs, incidents, or simple event data captured. With the amount of noise as well as the complexity of network environments, servers, applications, and remote devices, labor needs better intelligence to achieve a level of effectiveness required today. The tools needed must address security from a threat-intelligence perspective in order to assess incidents and events individually as well as relating them to activity within the entire environment of associated devices and applications in their network.

---

[13] Wikipidia.org SIEM - coined by Mark Nicolett and Amrit Williams of Gartner in 2005, SEM – Security Event Management, SIM – Security Information Management, terms often used interchangeably.

From Mundane to Useful Intelligence

The activity of security must pass all the way through the mundane and fundamental to the complex activities of monitoring, analyzing, and acting against threats. An example of moving past the mundane, and adding TK capital to labor, is the ever-increasing automation of penetration-testing software. The purpose of automation is so that less skilled staff can accomplish the more mundane but important aspects of it on their own, leaving the more skilled professional to guide and analyze the results of the process within the testing tool. Because Pen testing is a very complex activity, like many areas effecting security, it's more difficult to find qualified professionals. By applying automation to much of the basic prodding and results gathering the higher level professional can spend more quality time analyzing the results. It's an example of the direction necessary for technology to pick up areas where continually adding automation certain actions can be effective. Done correctly—to enhance professional proficiency—this type of capability could help ease the burden of the most difficult aspect of security, the volume of pedestrian, often useless data that can slow down and even cloud threat understanding and decision making. However, it can't replace the human factor, as that is the big "I" in threat Intelligence, primarily because the attackers are humans using their big "I" along with sophisticated tools to conduct their tasks.

Like penetration testing, better security can't be realized through the current methods of utilizing security professionals and systems in one-off deployments of single system silo's; there just aren't enough professionals to go around. The variety and number of systems further complicates staff shortages. As long as silos of network and security systems don't mesh together, they will continue to create complex security environments that are harder to manage. And they will continue to provide *threat actor's* with ripe opportunities to take advantage of the complexity and reap rich rewards.

For better or worse, a standard reality we can anticipate to continue is that all environments become more complex over time. As mentioned this certainly includes computing in all its aspects. This has been true of all sciences or most other human endeavors as well. From computing to bridge design, building, or farming, the field never grows towards simplicity but towards complexity; the base of human knowledge grows so that a new normal is always more complex than the last. This is clearly noticeable over the centuries. An example is the discovery of bacteria and viruses that led to the introduction of simple water treatment and waste-management systems, so cities were no longer breeding grounds for diseases like cholera. These systems are now common, and have become very complex and sophisticated environments that require a much higher amount of knowledge from designers and workers for them to function properly. Computing also drives the need to continually add to the available knowledge base. The difference with doing this within the security realm is it needs to do so at a level of immediacy because of the nature of its environment and the active threats it's uniquely subjected to. The results from active intelligence information along with new tools should enable professionals to scale their security capabilities to address current and future computing needs and complexity. A part of this is represented by TK, which is essentially digitizing labor by building a dynamically available knowledge base within a computing environment accessible to professionals as needed. It is the foundation that can help elevate the capabilities professionals need to bring to their jobs in order to address security now and in the future.

Utilizing software technology should support structuring baseline knowledge into threat intelligence so that protection can be more forward leaning. By being able to identify and then replicate security-scenarios-based activities, professionals can add capabilities to not only spot current threats but also to help anticipate them.

This means that smaller staff members can focus on the results coming from supportive systems and methodologies that help sort out noise and debris from real threat activities. This should help by delivering more dynamic situational awareness derived from deeper visibility and intelligence, threat tracking and analysis that can extract relevant activity from all the systems activity. This would be more of a continuous, proactive, and predictive protection ecosystem. Security professionals could work within the ecosystem to identify and maintain an acceptable risk profile through both automated and staff tuning of defenses based on the visibility derived from a continuous-threat scenario inspection and analysis intelligence framework.

The sorry fact is that it's very difficult to keep skillful hackers out of a network. So if you can't keep them out, you need to have the means to discover them getting in or being able to detect and investigate them while they are still in the system. Ideally, this would be best before they've grabbed the target information and left. One simple goal can be to make the cost or time needed for a hacker to succeed high enough to at least shut out the marginal hackers, so they will go after less sophisticated defenses. A problem with the marginal players is they create so much noise through their attack volume that they make it more difficult for staff to identify and catch the important players. Being able to reduce their noise level could be beneficial to security being able to spot the more dangerous hackers, who are good at hiding within all the noise.

IT Security Economy of Scale

In many situations, the lower the price is per unit, the more value you get for each additional unit at that price. This tends to be a standard expectation when purchasing many different products. Often, the next added good only creates marginal change to the areas in which they are used and don't tend to change or increase the complexity of the environment they will be used within. In the case of security, you may get a lower price per unit as you purchase more, but as more systems go in their ease of use and management is more of an inverse relationship to the numbers deployed. The more security an organization tends to add, the less value per unit it may provide. One reason for this is it can become more difficult to isolate or deal with the added traffic a marginal system may flag because of the additional noise and management complexity each new system can add to the current level. As you purchase more security, the base of systems grow because it's difficult for organizations to remove or throw away any deployed product. Most likely, existing products are replaced with another system by a competing company or a newer version of the original system from the same vendor. The end result tends toward more and more systems layered within various parts of a network, again adding to overall complexity.

The problem isn't that each one of these added security systems doesn't address some need; it's that as they add up, they introduce as many, if not more, problems than the actual individual solution may theoretically solve. In the world of security, traditional economies of scale work well for the security companies in their production of more and better security products, but not necessarily for organizations purchasing and deploying security products. Even with additional security products, the layering and sheer number of products may make for a less secure environment because they can unintentionally mask activities in a network with their added traffic generation.

Successful hacks have penetrated many computing environments with security systems that were properly deployed and maintained according to their specifications. Just because security meets regulatory or operational guidelines doesn't make it impervious; on the contrary, that can be another weakness. For example, during an exchange of data between a credit card and a card reader, companies can't be blamed for having the expectation that such a fundamental system won't be at risk from spear phishing or *zero-day attacks*. However, with so much overall network activity taking place, what may be thought of as a simple system, such as card readers, may mean their activities and need for protection disappears inside the din of other systems deemed more vulnerable. Devices like this are often left forgotten and vulnerable because they're not considered a risk due to their simplicity. Unfortunately, with all the security systems notifications and overall traffic noise, companies often don't note or simply can't tell whether simpler systems are covered, the result of this gap is unfortunately to pay the price from a successful attack.

Customized Network and Security Environments

The variety and complexity of network systems along with security solutions means, in essence, that everything done in security and networking has the aspects of a custom design and deployment. When you look at a wide variety of organizations, it's pretty easy to say that no two networks deployed are exactly alike, in fact they can differ quite a bit. The software, devices, and device combinations, along with the security used to protect all of the devices and their data, are never deployed exactly the same. This means that even when using best practices and similar solutions, unique issues will be built into each network environment. Many company networks may have similar equipment and similar applications and be deployed in a similar fashion, but none are ever exactly the same. It's really not feasible for any organization to think networks and security can be set up in a cookie cutter fashion. There are common-sense rules and standards professionals follow for network design and layout. At the same time each designer likes to use and deploy certain routers or switches, server platforms as well as applications and preferred security systems and vendors. This pushes customization, not yet counting the different departments that will want their own applications, servers, and end devices based on what they prefer and require.

Then these different departments also have their own network segment attached to the core network, perhaps enforcing unique policies for a different set of applications appropriate to their needs. In addition, there may be unique computing aspects to a department, such as finance, marketing, or human resources that further push towards a more customized network and also drives security requirements with more specialized capabilities. All this creates a mixture of systems, applications, and devices that are different for every organization. Security becomes all the more difficult as it is forced into being a custom patchwork of solutions to address these networks. The solutions will also likely come from multiple companies, meaning that along with every computing environment the attendant security is also a unique blend of products for each organization. So with every environment being special, security and IT staff must have specific skills for that particular site as well as acceptable tools they are can use or are authorized to purchase. And the entire set of security product, on top of a customized network setup, have often been implemented by staff that are often no longer with the organization. With existing staff, all of this makes it a tall order against which to succeed, to say the least, in order to ensure good security. Often what we see here is every department, including security, tries to do the best they can and often do as good a job as the situation will allow. Unfortunately this is far from an ideal point to ensure either a robust or a manageable security posture.

Better Amortization of Existing Security Investments

With all the different security systems already in place, it would seem a prudent goal would be to better utilize their threat information flows within a correlational intelligence analysis system. In review of the known breaches, it's safe to assume that in every case, security professionals were continually doing their best to identify and protect any critical exposure they subsequently identified. And during these evaluation exercises they of course used the information and tools they had on hand. When evaluating this entire scenario, it isn't that valuable information isn't being generated by security systems; it's just not very usable coming from so many sources, each with a unique context and variety of differing threat perspectives. Unfortunately, this is like trying to use a tool to assess a forest fire that only allows the viewer to see the overall conflagration—it misses fuel sources where the fire either started or that the fire can use to continue to spread.

In essence each individual security system tend to focus their observation to just a burning branch or blade of grass. Because systems have limits in their ability to inform other systems what they've observed means that a viewer is challenged to get a greater understanding of the impact of each individual fire to the overall conflagration. A forest fire—like threats—when viewed from thirty-thousand feet, looks like one single inferno. Upon closer inspection, however, it is a set of interrelated fires. The science is to understand how each one acts within the specific terrain they are burning and how they can be dealt with effectively within that area. This also has to include how a specific fire may feed or be a part of another fire area. In our context, the network is the terrain, and each fire is a threat point that needs to be seen and probed in order to gather enough information for an overall protection and response strategy, as well as a targeted threat response strategy when needed. To have a cohesive security strategy requires security acts judiciously in their attention and avoid getting caught up in fighting one burning twig at a time. You do, however, have to know how the twigs may be interrelated and where primary fuel sources are located to potentially intensify a fire (a fuel source could be the target within your network worth stealing so can intensify a hacker's activity). It is important to not lose details that can point to current or potential hot spots, at the same time, being able to fit all the little details and puzzles together to come up with an overall defense and threat containment strategy.

With security, the only way to really amortize a current investment in each security product is to increase each individual product's contribution by extracting more value from the information the various security solutions provide. This isn't going to happen by adding more security solutions or by expecting the ones you have to provide additional information in a more usable format than what they already provide. Every solution has its capabilities and limitations, and security professionals have to determine how to better use the information solutions they already have. As mentioned before, many related events can be noted by different security systems. These events aren't necessarily flagged because each system only sees one part of an activity and aren't designed to connect multiple activities outside of its rule set. Greater insight into these events can take place when comparing them within an overall threat-analysis system to access information from all of the stand-alone systems and parlaying that into greater visibility and threat intelligence.

This whole exercise is to make better use of flows to create big data threat capture, correlation and analysis. It could associate bodies of information from all the divergent systems to effectively isolate actual threats or critical events from the noise. Analysts would be able to gather specific information as the result of big data processing that could help quickly point to threat areas that the analyst can then conduct a more detailed review on a case by case basis as needed. As with penetration testing organizations utilize when attempting to determine how hackers may get into their network, using big data can help security professionals by producing better threat indicator activities. Taken further, this could even help identify hackers preferred techniques used in their attacks. Being able to have greater intelligence on any particular hacker an organization may see more than once, means the organization can develop a defense based on intelligence on a hacker, their techniques and what they tend to be after. This can only help improve an organizations defensive posture and response capabilities.

Often the best reaction to a threat is a semi-customized one based on a solid foundation of responses. It's unfortunately not sensible to expect canned response actions against an attack on one part of the network's terrain to necessarily be appropriate for dealing with another type of attack at other points in a network. This is largely derived from a foundation of responses analysts can build that incorporates proven response sequences and methodologies. The methodologies have to include the systems they use and techniques that they follow to deal with each unique situation. Just as the network and security is custom, so is each attack, and so within parameters should be a defense. This requires accessing centralized information and being able to quickly extract and correlate the threat or threat types being seen at this juncture so an appropriate response can be quickly assembled. This could be used to develop an information map with potential responses from existing systems. The design would be to allow the expert to identify overarching patterns and drill down further to find the data sources leading to the initial or ongoing threat activity. Even though silo systems do have valuable information in this context, organizations need to utilize a broader body of information to quickly and effectively address the fleeting nature of the process most attacks take. The fact is attackers will do their best to spend as little time as possible in order to get their work done. Unless it's clear to a hacker they have all the time they need and can do as they please. In that case an organization is really in trouble, and unfortunately they likely won't even know it unless an attacker has become so brazen that they end up exposing their presence.

Chapter 4

We Can Solve That Problem. Just Add...

In the security industry, the noise continues to grow regarding how many vendor's state their products can identify, capture, block, find, and detonate a threat, for instance in some form of a processing environment that can isolate the threat and execute it. The goal for the industry of course is to make sure all data within any organization is safe and effectively protected. The promise that's been made for years is to be able to guard against viruses, malware, targeted attacks, distributed denial of service (DDoS), infiltration, exfiltration, ransomware, advanced persistent threats (APT) and others—all these are either older threat types or more recently identified types of threat activities. The industry is still in somewhat of a "wild west" phase in terms of solutions that provide broad capabilities for systematic threat visibility within a network. The good news is that companies are beginning to recognize this need and moving closer toward this capacity.

Some companies with more traditional type of protection technologies and product focus are just starting to admit the overarching issues a product's narrow view brings to protection effectiveness. A few are attempting to address the narrowness of their existing product view in a variety of different ways. This can be the addition of new features to existing product, buying a company for a new product, conducting a thorough product redesign or designing and coding an entirely new product. Most companies, based on their existing engineering capabilities and product revenue, will tend to stay within a similar design and protection orientation as products they've already succeeded with. Just like many other areas, there is a comfort zone organizations tend to stay within regardless of any insurmountable evidence stating the opposite and the need to diverge from their current norm.

The available mountain of information needs to be scaled so it can produce intelligence that allows analysts to derive a robust and actionable picture of an organizations specific device and overall threat posture. And along with that, provides the ability for analyst and security personnel to validate and act on the information their seeing, quickly and decisively.

In looking at a depiction or simple (and I use the term simple loosely here) map of the Internet, with its endless number of connection points and available paths, it becomes evident how difficult having visibility within that world can be. Putting any one organization's network within the context of this map, no matter how large that organization's network may be, it would be totally lost in the picture. It's seems an impossible task for organization's to try to identify, at any point in time, all their network links to the Internet. And, if an organization has a large network, it can be equally daunting to determine exactly all their own internal links and paths. If, for various reasons, their own links are constantly changing, how can an organization feel confident it can protect entry into its network at every potential point of Internet contact, and, in conjunction, protect every point within its network?

This question is compounded further when taking into account BYOD devices, custom network design, custom security deployment, thousands of applications and users as well as other customizations that become part of an overall network picture. An image of the complexity can be a comparison of an accomplished video gamer playing within a multilayer game that has endless layers to contend with at once. In addition, the weaponry of their opponents during the game is always changing, and the opponent can continually apply different strategies not visible to the player. On top of this impossible scenario, the player is unable to tell where their opponents are firing at them from, or for that matter, whether they're even firing or not at any given moment. The kicker is that the opponent can always tell where the player is, but the video gamer has no means to ascertain much if any information about the opponent, such as even whether it's a single or multiple opponents their dealing with. Obviously, it's a bit of a tilted game. When one sees the complexity an Internet map represents, it's impressive that security has done as well as it has; however, now security and business-technology professionals need to step up to developing security 2.0 because advanced threats along with advanced threat actors have been tilting the game into their own court.

The continuing dependence on networked computing systems means that all data has some level of risk to exposure. No matter how well defended, the risk will never be zero. Since there is no point in having or creating data of no value or if you aren't going to use it, exposure will always be the rule, not the exception. Simply because there is something of value to take, and there will always be those willing to take it, risk can't be eliminated. Clearly the benefit of computing technology, hardware, software, connectivity, data creation, manipulation, access, and sharing gives societies far more positive returns than the negative issues being discussed here.

As in any complex and growing body, whether flesh and blood or bits in silicon chips, it's clear that there will always be those who try to benefit from manipulating a target body in a manner that circumvents the host's desire or intention. These are the threats that are parasitical to computing and have no concern for whether the host or its branches thrive or even survive. Like any drug or physical regimen to address physical health, there is no silver bullet to protect against ill intention from avaricious players. The essence or protection must either be some means of isolating the capacity for a nasty player to conduct his or her work, at least within an organizations domain, reducing their returns for the work involved, or simply destroying their capability to take or damage what society values.

Today, most security products are fundamentally disconnected from each other. The tendency is organizations hope that the next single product can effectively combat the problems that arise from cyber aggression and theft that a current product doesn't address. The continuous creation of the many single products with the expectation that they can solve problems outside of their design scope is akin to a person suffering from appendicitis and going to an optometrist for a cure. Even though an optometrist is a certified and skilled professional, he or she likely won't have the knowledge to diagnose the problem, let alone treat it. Any specialty, such as in medicine, can miss the big picture by looking at just one part of the body. To build a whole-body picture in security means that all of the systems are connected and that the information they all generate is first shared and then can be utilized in order to get whole-body protection.

The sale of security products from thousands of companies is a good indicator of the nature of the problems facing users, organizations and developers. For example, 2013 sales of cybersecurity software totaled $67.2 billion worldwide according to Gartner,[14] which was up by 8.7 percent from the 2012 amount of $61.8 billion. Also according to Gartner, the expectation for global growth in total sales by 2016 is forecast to hit $86 billion. This represents nearly 30 percent in revenue growth in less than three years—heady growth for any industry. Predictions are that this level of growth won't slow down anytime soon, particularly when you take into

[14] Gartner 2013 June 10-13 Gartner Security Risk & Management Summit at National Harbor, MD

account the "Internet of Things" (IoT). The IoT is bringing an even greater number of devices and systems into the fold, with various links to the Internet and organizations networks that drives the need for some level of protection. Based on research—and note I could not get definitive numbers—my estimate is there are well over ten-thousand security companies globally, with perhaps hundreds of new ones being funded in Silicon Valley and other parts of the world every year. These companies are specifically oriented towards different aspects and niche areas of cybersecurity, further indicating that there are a lot of security opportunities (or gaps) that existing companies have and new startups are attempting to fill. Of course, this is both a good news, bad news scenario. It's great that gaps are being identified and there are companies trying to fill them, but it's terrible there are gaps and more companies and products have to be built to try and contain them.

There are real business opportunities that are being identified by today's security industry; unfortunately, the overall picture continues to layer on more security systems, increasing complexity along with the increased network volume to sort out. These new solutions, like many traditional ones, have value but don't look like they will do much more than continue to patch weak areas. This is a constant filling in the gaps left by many of today's security systems. And even when the new systems provide value, there is still the continuous lament of how the new systems add to the already abundant noise and further cluttering of information. And in the attempt to take advantage of gap opportunities by adding new types of solutions that can introduce new gaps, and the cycle continues.

As one would expect, each company presents its system capabilities to users through a user interface that is often unique to each product offering. Unfortunately, this is even within a single company that has multiple product offerings. This is a bit crazy for the poor IT or security professional who has to deal with each different user interface. As mentioned, layering is used to try to match the network and systems growth step by step, with accompanying points of protection, like building an onion from the outside in. This technique is like inserting pieces of protective tin foil between each layer of the onion so that if one layer is fouled, the foil can keep it from impacting other layers. In this area, a lack of UI consistency between solutions can impact how that security system displays the available knowledge about what it may be telling them now, particularly in comparison to other products.

Because layering security products has been largely piecemeal and custom as systems are added along with devices and applications, the price paid for the customization is usually visibility and readily available network intelligence. For instance, the large breach in 2013 at Target did have high-level notifications from a well-regarded APT solution that there was a critical problem needing immediate attention. The security staff wasn't able to act on the notices as they didn't understand or distinguish their significance from all the rest of the noise they were dealing with. Unfortunately this is an all too common issue. In this case, the tool was there, but the result of poor implementation, training, or a simple lack of attention and response resulted in severe brand damage, people fired, and $146 million in expense-related costs.[15]

There have been many other major breaches at retailers and other companies of a similar nature, such as Home Depot in Sept 2014[16] that had similar modes of failure. These are all prime examples of the overwhelming complexity of the security environment and the ongoing noise any network creates. All of this clearly impacts

[15] USA Today August 20, 2014
[16] Krebs on Security http://krebsonsecurity.com/2014/09/banks-credit-card-breach-at-home-depot/

company security personnel's ability to notice and identify any kind of threat. This is particularly when the agents of the threat know how the defender works along with what tools they use so that they can take advantage of the target's harried environment to mask their activities.

This reflects a big problem for many organizations—the countless incident or event notifications from all their deployed systems. For a variety of reasons, such as the volume of events, limited time to pay attention to details, busy schedules, and understaffing, the unfortunate companies breached weren't able to separate critical elements from ongoing noise or which critical element should be immediately addressed. This was even though alerts were from a system designed to do just that—provide focused, high-priority information alerts for immediate attention by security. Since that system only gave limited critical alerts, it meant they had an immediate problem if it provided an alert. Unfortunately, organizations still have trouble distinguishing what is critical, even when it's clear that a particular system has elevated an issue from everything else. In the case of Target and Home Depot, they got "data". No one seemed to appreciate the risk those alerts indicated because it wasn't seen as intelligence; it was treated as another data alert to be dealt with when they had the time. It seems clear that as security professionals, they may have lost the contextual framework of what was going on for many reasons. For instance, from the monotony of network traffic noise, they may have grown immune to being able to notice more important warnings.

Having trouble sorting out important information from a lot of extraneous noise is not unusual. There have been studies done in hospitals that show similar issues with all of the alerts staff are subjected to. These were done specifically regarding all the beeping alerts and alarms going off in any patient setting. Over time, it becomes so noisy that medical staff members often fail to notice key alerts where missing them could have gloomy consequences. In that setting, there are ways organizations are trying to deal with the clamor by socially engineering the environment to address the need of getting a staff person's attention for a critical alert without bombarding them with yet more noise. This, obviously, is not an easy task.

How does an organization categorize an issue on the fly while it's busy trying to keep its network operational and protected against the roar of constant threats? And that roar is the fact that any organization can easily get hits on its systems by attempted hackers hundreds of times a day, and often much more. The problem lies both with evidence and information. There is clearly overwhelming evidence of activities both good and bad taking place, along with masses of business content, information, and other data traversing a network. The process of trying to sniff out any evidentiary threat information has to be dealt with differently than standard business information. It might be that the organization structure of security and IT departments must be brought into consideration. Accounting for different cultural ecosystems within which a department may operate may need to be reviewed as to how that may impact the ability to do the job. Most of these organizations basically structure around the systems they deploy and manage in a hierarchical manner. Perhaps that needs to change because systems designed to extract and process data for the purpose of creating broader threat intelligence need to work across all department lines for both gathering and responding to the intelligence. In addition, can an organizational structure make it easier for key parties to have a better picture of what is currently transpiring? This would include the overall health of systems, current threat activity, and access to a complete threat posture of the entire environment, not just each individual department or group section.

Like individual systems, security personnel deal within an organization structure that can be so specialized and segmented that no one can get a complete picture of all systems and activities. This may mean reviewing security and IT organizations to determine whether they ought to be restructured to better meet the needs of the job they have to do today. And if a new structure is considered, it needs to be flexible enough to deal with the constantly morphing environment of systems and threats. This would be in contrast to trying to maintain a static methodology and expecting it to have the flexibility to address more dynamic threats. At the same time, a dynamic ability needs to be associated with a foundation of static knowledge and capabilities as well, so a combination of both environments is more the order of the day.

Chapter 5

Classifying Information

It seems that classifying information—for instance, according to its importance—is a simple problem to address. It is, on the surface, except for obvious and not-so-obvious fundamental issues that have been causing nightmares for every organization on the planet for years. First off, the sheer amount of data or information any organization has to deal with on a daily basis, as well as what could accumulate over time is overwhelming. This one issue can continuously stress operating and storage environments because it forces the continuous addition of new systems and applications that have to deal with all the data. Not to mention the continual load on staff's ability to manage all these different systems and applications for storing and manipulating data. As a consideration of the overall volume organizations have to deal with globally, just a couple of years into the twenty-first century, a milestone were achieved; the amount of data generated in a single year was greater than all the data created by the human race throughout our history. According to SINTEF[17] which is the largest independent research organization in Scandinavia, in 2013, 90 percent of the entire world's data has been generated over the last two years. This rate of data creation indicates that the mass of data generation will likely continue to eclipse itself for the foreseeable future.

Of course, with that data generation there is also a colossal capacity to store and move data around. When one considers the volume constantly in motion becomes an enormous logistical and managerial problem. In addition, if the data is moved, how does

[17] Science Daily, 22 May 2013. <www.sciencedaily.com/releases/2013/05/130522085217.htm>

the organization know for sure where their most valuable data resides? Considering the aspect of sensibly classifying all this data so that it can be properly stored according to its value as well as readily available creates all kinds of challenges. All the logistics, data management, and security issues turn into a maelstrom of globally flying bits that are difficult to get under any semblance of control. The data just moves, shifts, disappears, and resurfaces in the blink of a keystroke. Estimates by researchers at the University of Southern California in an article published in *Science Express* on September 10, 2011 stated that there were approximately 295 exabytes (295 billion gigabytes) of storage capacity globally, with capacity doubling every three years to around 600 exabytes in 2014—a whole lot of capacity with a whole lot of data. And that number likely woefully understates reality. And there wasn't any means for the researchers to exactly quantify whether every byte was taken up. Conservatively assuming that storage utilization is at a constant 60 percent to 70 percent of capacity, this means that in 2014, a conservative estimate was over 400 exabytes of data in storage with a large portion during any period of time traversing the global network. This is a lot of stuff, most of which is very important to an individual or organization as well as to everyone on the planet in some form since it basically supports the continued existence of local and global society.

Data Is Everything and Everywhere

Data about you; your company; your children, pets, and relatives; your living environment and habits; and information about organizations, systems, and just general information resides within accessible storage located in all kinds of places. Credit card information, personal identification on a driver's license, health care, membership cards with information from thousands of business frequent user award systems are a few examples. Data can be stored on local POS systems for a period of time during a transaction, then a local server, and sent at some point to a corporate server application and financial institution for further processing. Perhaps the data is also up loaded to a corporate data center, backed up to another site, perhaps via a third party or to a cloud located out of the country of origin. An organization may process the information within their site or may use a contract system for this as well as its storage, or storage could be yet another supplier. The chain of movement, processing and storage that can take place at any given time for a body of data is labyrinthine. On the face of it, this seems to be continually intertwining sets of data movement within shifting organizational relationships with no beginning or end once the first keystroke or card read takes place.

And much data is dealt within cloud environment frameworks where processing time and capability is purchased as needed, so data is subjected to quickly being moved between systems and locations. The cloud can also be part of local processing as a hybrid environment where some processing or storage takes place in an organizations data center or hosted systems in a provider's data center as well as in contracted cloud processing at various locations. At the same time data is being actively processed, it can reside on individual PCs or BYOD devices, all in various states of use and alteration. It can also be e-mailed, meaning it may be stored on e-mail servers and backups or saved to another local drive or a portable USB stick or some other external storage. At the same time an individual that is working with some data, could also have another person (or many other people) working with some part or a version of the same data at another location. As is the case with most business as they operate on a global scale, the workday ends when the task is done, not when the clock strikes a particular time. Along with the global reach of a connection with any device, pretty much all data is now accessible from anywhere at any time by someone, whether authorized or not.

The scenario isn't complete without data being outsourced to a foreign country for processing and storage. For example a foreign entity computing a medical bill with the results sent back to a local billing or processing center to do the final bill to the client to complete its data processing lifecycle. Outsourced medical analysis work, for instance, done in India, where a US doctor can send X-rays or an MRI for initial evaluation with the results sent back to them within twenty-four hours. All of this data is sent through a shared network system, across routers and lines the sending or receiving company doesn't own and can't control. And, if there is a problem during sending, it would be difficult to trace the data's path at any given time. If analyzed data didn't arrive, the solution is to simply resend the information. Everyone can encrypt data to better ensure protection during transit, hoping that both receiving parties are diligent in keeping the keys safe. Unfortunately, there is always a threat of data being stolen by an internal source, so encrypting will help very little against authorized access. There is a lot of data in a lot of places with many access points and many opportunities by many players who would be difficult to identify; no wonder there are successful hacks.

Security's Complex Capabilities Impact Its Value

A comical comparison of what computer security is faced with today would be to a theme park game you may be familiar with: whack-a-mole. To add a bit of complexity to this game, imagine that you need to use a whole array of hammers to address different type and size of hole. At the same time, each hammer has a learning curve for its most efficient use that is also unique to each individual hole a hammer is to be used for. In this scenario, in order to ready its defenses for the next head popping out of a hole, the security industry tries to bring ever bigger, faster, more sophisticated and varied hammers to address the rapidity of moles heads popping up. These hammers continually offer specialized expertise within a narrow realm of their special threat capabilities as required by each unique hole. This means there is a learning curve in the proper use of any hammer, let alone a new, more powerful and complex one. By the time one learns how to swing the "right" hammer on the "right" hole, the mole has popped up and back down and is on their merry way to the next hole. The questions that arise every time is how to select which hammer is the best one to use next time a mole starts to emerge, and how can one be ready to swing it at the correct moment and at the correct hole?

Any delay in reaction to swing the hammer probably means that the mole has already been down in the network and data dungeons ingesting information. However, if you swung the wrong hammer, potentially at the wrong hole, you have no idea whether this incorrect action might obfuscate determining whether a mole had been there at all anyway. The adage is unfortunately prevalent in this case: If the only tool you have is a hammer, then everything looks like a nail. Unfortunately these are smart nails.

The case that security has normally been reactive doesn't mean we shouldn't consider creating tools that provide a better opportunity to interrupt any hidden activity of the mole. The conundrum is if a mole is poking its head out of a hole how can we somehow grab hold of its feet from below so we're no longer concerned with it popping back down before we can hit it. If we can somehow grab it by the feet we can simply push its little ass from the bottom up through the hole, with the luxury of time we now have to select the right tool and give it a good old whack. This takes visibility and threat intelligence.

So, in the simplest words, instead of just whacking the mole, we need to be able to both anticipate and then suspend what it may be doing so that it can't wildly rummage through data. This could be done in the interim until a full scenario is considered and appropriate actions and protection put in place to get rid of it and close any avenues it may have been using. Too often, security tools are looking at shadows of movement, and applying the closest hammer available. This may provide some points of reference to start from but often means a hacker has already moved into your systems, forcing defenders to chase there shadows blindly down multiple mole holes.

As mentioned in chapter 2, there are thousands of different security systems, types, and variations that organizations can implement to protect computing environments. According to the SANS Institute,[18] there are over seven-hundred terms or concepts associated with security listed in their glossary of security terms. Interestingly it may be reasonable to consider the number of terms a loose indicator of the potential number and variety of security systems. Consider a security professional's need to know or understand the characteristics of these terms and how they may apply to their job. In addition to these terms, each individual company will have its own terms and concepts as they relate to their own security solutions, policies and procedures. Then add the terms and concepts that are also unique to a particular vendor or product set. Add to this the categories of professional roles, security training, certifications, and specialization with those concepts. These are all in the name of trying to provide the foundations for a deep understanding of specific areas so that an individual can become an expert within that category. However, with specialization comes the unfortunate fact that as a person becomes more highly specialized they can tend to lose the all-inclusive view of the entire security and network ecosystem. This creates individuals that tend to fit the silo product model of a particular area of security. These people are smart enough for broader views. The difficult part is there aren't yet the tools to help

---

[18] http://www.sans.org/security-resources/glossary-of-terms/?pass=c

take them beyond the silo to a more inclusive network security ecosystem.

A silo orientation in both products and solutions thinking can weaken organizations' ability to develop an attitude that can consider necessary elements for a more adaptable defensive posture. This can impact security planning capabilities along with the need for continuous threat adjustment—as a dynamic defense can be tuned to the threat events or assessments of the day.

An example of potential jobs categorized as elements of security that show how silo type training can come about from specific security roles needs. This is compiled by the SANS Institute in their "20 Cool Infosec & Cybersecurity Jobs,"[19] known as the SANS 20. These are categories that allow SANS and other organizations to offer a rich set of accompanying educational courses for training and certification in those areas. These types of courses provide clear value to organizations and their staff, but because of their focus, they may limit some thinking due to a fundamental complexity within the security environment they're trying to train for. There may be simply too much for any one individual to know. Until systems can help add to a broader intelligence view, this isn't likely to get any better. It isn't that organizations such as SANs and many others aren't doing a good job, they're a valuable organization for security and training. It's more around the nature of the complexity and difficulty of the subject and humans tendency to continually segment knowledge into ever smaller specializations as the base of knowledge increases. This is not an unreasonable thing to do. It may be that for security purposes it's a poor methodology to deal with increasingly complex threat environments. This also gets back to reviewing how security and IT could be organized in order to help mitigate the ongoing issue of specialization. Whatever the

---

[19] http://www.sans.org/20coolestcareers/

view, it's clearly not going away any time soon. Below is the SANs list of specialization training and certification categories available:

1. Information Security Crime Investigator/Forensics Expert
2. System, Network, and/or Web Penetration Tester
3. Forensic Analyst
4. Incident Responder
5. Security Architect
6. Malware Analyst
7. Network Security Engineer
8. Security Analyst
9. Computer Crime Investigator
10. CISO/ISO or Director of Security
11. Application Penetration Tester
12. Security Operations Center Analyst
13. Prosecutor Specializing in Information Security Crime
14. Technical Director and Deputy CISO
15. Intrusion Analyst
16. Vulnerability Researcher/Exploit Developer
17. Security Auditor
18. Security-Savvy Software Developer
19. Security Maven in an Application Developer Organization
20. Disaster Recovery/Business Continuity Analyst/Manager

For better or worse, professionals, by definition, become their own vertical silo of special knowledge. This has a great many benefits, but a price is it can also construct blind spots within the depth of specialized knowledge, which is true for any profession. In many areas, this may not be critical. To aspects of a security threat that doesn't trigger the specialized skill or fit within received training, can have potentially catastrophic results. And these gaps can be, and are, exploited by skilled threat actors, who are not limited by the same constraints of defenders. Attackers have the advantage of being able to approach a target problem horizontally and benefit by being able to look at all possible entry and exit points, as well as required actions once inside a target. They can test against many of the elements of a security infrastructure over time in order to identify their favored exploit points and follow on actions. And in today's complex organizational and computing structures, with silos of systems and expertise along with thousands of security solutions, entry and hiding places are always to be found.

There are many other defined categories besides what SANS covers that are unique within organizations and other educational and training entities that create solution as well as role- and product-specific training. There is great value in training and certifications for security professionals, with US educational organizations being some of the best in the world.

Big Data, Cloud, and Virtualization

Big data is historically characterized by the three V's: the extreme volume of data, the wide variety of types of data, and the velocity at which the data must be processed. The purpose of utilizing this in relation to security is to help uncover hidden patterns, unknown correlations, threat market trends, customer activities, or any information that could be useful for better security. With security in particular, processing speed that can find, identify (at least as something warranting quarantine or further analysis) and respond to a present or potential attack or security event is of high value. Utilizing different combinations of local and remote high-speed communication and processing power that is available from a cloud environment for big data may help reduce the time to discovery and speed of reaction. Also, maximizing protection for security purposes would seem to be prudent by having any remote processing environment contained, either within an organizations own private cloud or some other control method. Although big data doesn't refer to any specific quantity, the term is often used when speaking about petabytes and exabytes of data.

Various developments in computing have turned security on its head. Areas such as BYOD massively increase the exposure points security has to deal with to maintain its protection. In the positive light, the ability to gather huge bodies of information that may have seemed trivial before, in addition to clearly important information, and analyze it all was not possible until you could throw a lot of computing power at it. Now massive computing power along with robust well written algorithms can be used to identify important elements veiled within the volumes of available data. This could allow a security professional the opportunity to get the kinds of insight into their systems activity that wasn't possible a few years ago. Unfortunately, these same capabilities are also available to adversaries, however, not necessarily the same rich sets of data. The best of the hacker community are quite skilled at taking advantage of the overwhelming processing power now available, whether by contract or by force (botnet). Now everyone, including hackers, have access to big data sets to further identify and refine their activities. In the case of hackers or course this is in order to better target their efforts at an already beleaguered audience.

"Big data" tends to be the term to describe any voluminous amount of structured, semi structured, and unstructured data that has the potential to be mined for information.[20] One must note here that, by definition, it doesn't restrict access to this content only to the good guys. Anyone can build up or access big-data stores and utilize any results of their analysis for a lot of different activities. Cloud systems that are used for processing are just a computing resource that happens to have its processing utilized for a particular activity, such as for big data analysis of specified content. The cloud itself doesn't determine what any data may be used for; it just follows the instructions given to it for processing the data based on a contract, as long as payment is being kept up to date by a

---

[20] http://searchcloudcomputing1.techtarget.com/definition/big-data-Big-Data

client, or if something is clearly out-of-bounds they will continue to process the data.

The aspect of processing or manipulating a big data store isn't concerned or doesn't make any specification of what type of information may or may not be set up to be mined. The application of big-data gathering and analysis for security is as relevant as any data store. Being able to conduct massive correlation within a threat data set may help gain greater depth of understanding of an overall threat environment as well as to help spot specific threats. Being able to determine what should make up the content for analysis within a security orientation is important to help identify and then extract relevant information during processing. Depending on what is within that content as well as what criteria are used and applied for an analysis methodology can impact whether enough or anything of value can be pulled from the content. Security-related systems traffic patterns, logs, events, noted incidents and standard or unusual traffic flows compared against existing traffic standards can all be part of an organization's analysis and are example content that can be mined in order to try and gain some insight into a network's threat environment.

Classification and Categorization of Data

A significant attack that took place that resulted in exfiltration of key data, films, and company and personal information from e-mails was that of a major film studio in 2014. This event received much embarrassing international attention for the company. The backdrop of how they had managed their data tells an unfortunate story as to how badly an organization could address a critical aspect of simple data protection with a data-classification system that afforded basic content and file protection. The confounding aspect of this story is that this same organization had a very visible attack conducted against another division three to four years prior to the more recent one. The first attack cost a tremendous amount in both brand damage and cleanup costs, yet here they were again. In this case, it was even worse, as it seems that no one had applied what had been learned from the previous hacking lesson.

It would be great if we could look at an event like this as an anomaly and assume that most companies that have an initial issue will rigorously study and address the issues. Another hope would be that in an organizations review processes, they would fix their overall environment so that when another attack happened, they could have a better chance of identifying it early enough. Or, at a minimum an organization was prepared enough to be able to minimize damage and quickly contain the attack; unfortunately, that was just not the case. People have been fired, experts have made their analysis of what and how it happened, pundits have made their warnings and prognostications, and the public has shown its due concern. Yet business continues as usual, without enough of a big-picture analysis so efforts can be brought to the forefront to help ensure that when an organization is penetrated, they have a better chance of discovering it.

According to *Bloomberg Business Week*, in an article about this particular attack in their Companies/Industries[21] section, a quote by the chief of the studio stated that it wasn't "anyone's fault who works here." Understanding that this company didn't hack themselves and that it looks to have been a state sponsored attack, to be realistic it would have been difficult or impossible for any organization to defend against. The fact that the hackers seemed to have free rein of the network for so long leaves one to ask what anyone there was thinking and what preparation had been done to spot an attack. The hackers were able to take a huge amount of sensitive information that was stored in plaintext, even though it clearly should have been encrypted and stored in a secure area.

---

[21] Bloomberg Business Week December 22-28, page 20

For example, a file called "publicity bibles" had celebrity's aliases and other personal data. Another file cleverly called "passwords" contained exactly what you would expect in a file of that name. This seemed like institutional blindness to the risks regarding so much important information without any consideration of ramifications or consequences if there were to be a breach. The clear lack of accounting for the difference in importance between different data, such as passwords, means it was pretty much impossible to provide any level of security for that information, no matter how hard a security organization may try to ensure against any initial penetration or to discover a hacker once they're in.

Once in, finding areas of interest would have been easy when there is simply no appropriate data classification for what is undoubtedly sensitive information. In this case, hopefully a minimal security education and enforced policies could have had its place by making sure parties who owned this data understood and followed a set of rules that recognized the sensitivity of some data and the need for it to be treated that way. If anything, ensuring every person in an organization follows a reasonable set of procedures to maintain critical data to have a level of understanding that their activities impact organizations' ability to protect valuable resources could be a start. As mentioned before, and these attacks continue to prove, it isn't a matter of whether a hacker will get in, but a matter of when. One must be prepared, starting at the foundation of how information is classified and stored as well as who has access to it.

The question becomes how to ensure that when a hacker gets in, you can minimize any damage or removal of sensitive data because it is stored within an area that further restrains access to it based on its intrinsic value, as well as being named in a way to reduce its visibility. Without disparaging the security staff at this organization as they couldn't help but fail based on who attacked them, the poor choice in file naming convention meant the opportunity for damage was ripe. This particular attack seemed more like a teenage son and his friends taking a brand new Tesla out for a drive and beating the hell out of it, with dents, broken glass, torn and burnt seats, and flat tires. Yet, as only a teenager could do, they were able to get it home and then plug it in to the charging system. Then in the morning, the teen's father and owner of the car checked out the charging station and were pleased when they saw that the charge indicator light showed that the car was fully charged, without checking any other aspect of the vehicle. This particular hacking event is another hard lesson on how not to develop a secure data mindset. Having this mindset, from the top to the bottom of an organization is the only way to have a safe environment. That means applying rules and policies to make sure that this mindset is applied across the board for the most to least important data.

With all that, a simple baseline for security is the well-defined and continuous classification and categorization of data, including location. The ability for continuous inspection and analysis of devices, traffic, and activity so that defenders can continuously adjust their defense as needed should also be included. This is necessary because the attacker is constantly adjusting their attack. There needs to be an information map built for data containment that covers classification, categorization, and access as one of the many foundation elements for good data security. If you don't know where your data is, who can access it, what systems and applications have access, where it has gone, and who has or can see it, it doesn't matter how good your security is; the data is flying naked in the wind, and it's just a matter of time before a hacker raises a sail to capture it.

Chapter 6

Attack Surfaces

Fundamental System and Data Protection

E very organization can ensure that its systems and data is secure by never turning on any computing device. If the company members also run all of their computing systems through a physical crusher, particularly any storage disk, that is likely to assure the data will be safe forever. But, of course, it won't be particularly usable for an organization or anyone else, so that's a pretty absurd option. Without the computing capability we have today, most, if not all, organizations would not be able to function, certainly not at the level of today's organizational sophistication. Even if everyone learned how to use an abacus or typewriter in order to create and use data, the ramifications would be rather dire. Even these simple devices weren't without risk. All communication and created data are at risk regardless of efforts to protect or mask what is being created and shared. The goal is to arrive at a level of controllable risk that delivers greater benefits than the risk. It's a matter of gaining a better balance for data in the form of lowering its risk while still being widely assessable by many entities.

Without computing systems as the pulsing fabric of modern capabilities, our organizations and societies couldn't exist as they do today. This is also true as to the size of the global population. In relation to the age of human civilization, electronic computing is very new, less than 100 years old. The impact of computing as it has been put into mass use in every avenue of global and local societies is nothing short of astounding. When you compare electronic computing's short lifespan to the existence of civilization for over five-thousand years, it's a mere dash of time in overall human history. Based on the newness of electronic computing to societies, it might be good to take a broader look with deeper deliberation as to how computing resources are currently applied. The purpose would be to determine ways to better progress and enhance these resources as applicable to current and future human endeavors. Everything in the computing sphere that's been done up to this point has been pretty much ad hoc, including the security industry. This is not a criticism as it's more of the normal environment for growth in any complex human endeavor. Complex systems are normally built incrementally on a foundation of previous ongoing technical innovation. As the intensity of combined innovation takes place society changes in response to the types and volume of innovation involved. The circle of changes created fundamentally impacts how a society will apply them to exercise its job of survival. Thus, the ad hoc system that tends to be the rule of life, in many instances has worked quite well. Though there have been many areas where this has failed. And failure is part of the learning process, however at times at a very high cost. And most failures come primarily when unforeseen consequences of a single or combination of innovations are applied in some fashion and undesirable outcomes have not been considered. Obviously considering future potential consequences is a tough thing to attempt in any area, let alone something like security that can change so quickly and dramatically.

Initial networking system design did not start out with a focus on the long-term aspects of interconnecting the multitude of devices together that exist today. There wasn't a set of deliberate foundations of thought for what was the future network ecosystem being created. And there also wasn't initial concern for a computing environment that could ensure data integrity. All of this has taken place well after the entire computing environment fundamentals were already established and was rapidly moving forward. Initial computing design primary focus was to connect a narrow number of user or organizations systems and exchange documents between them. As most of the original parties working within the early generation of the environment were thus known to each other needing to incorporate a foundation for data integrity wasn't necessary as trust was already established. Along with ubiquitous connectivity and the unlimited numbers of devices and users that come with IoT charging out of the shadows adds more strain to organizations overall ability to ensure data integrity. A question to ask is whether it's feasible to consider starting over and build a new baseline that begins with the notion of data integrity. The fact is that a redesign just isn't possible. The overlying question then becomes what can be done to address the need to ensure data integrity while knowing the underlying structure has many unintentional and unforeseen gaps in its ability to support it in the first place?

Always On and Everywhere Data Exposure

The vast majority of computing equipment, whether a system directly accessed and used by humans or accessed by other systems without direct human interaction, are generally on all the time with short periods for maintenance or replacement. This essentially means that most devices attack "surfaces" are always available and can be targeted regardless of their current activity, business hours or otherwise. And their *attack surfaces* increase via connections to them from obscure devices within network environments or outlier "bring your own devices" (BYOD). Often the BYOD devices will have some means of access to other devices whether originally intended to be the case or not. And then there are computing devices that are rarely touched and pose a risk just because they are often forgotten and overlooked. For instance, individual systems may not expose much of an attack surface, but a large number of systems, such as POS types discussed earlier, can provide a wide attack surface that is difficult to secure. A couple of very successful hacks in the last few years have painfully pointed this out.

Besides physical systems, there are also virtual systems that are in heavy use today. Unlike systems of the past, whether you've turned off a specific virtual server or its application, traffic is still passing through the host machine even if a virtual server is in a dormant state. This can still expose a virtual platform with a dormant application to being hacked. Also, in virtual systems, each one running on a host can communicate with every other virtual system on that host. That means that if one virtual system is infiltrated, all the others are exposed to being infiltrated as well. Without yet another security system specific to virtual systems, they're all vulnerable. As is the case for all systems, but perhaps even more with virtual types, it's not as evident if a virtual system has been hacked. So, does this mean yet another security layer for each virtual system? This, of course, can further grow the complexity of the security environment, while not being clear whether another added layer has enough benefit to offset the increase in management overhead and complexity. Risk and overall operational restraints must be balanced against any benefits that may be derived from yet another layer.

Any good hacker will do his or her best to make sure an alert is not triggered indicating their penetration to compromise a system by often first disabling protection software. The risk of this may be greater because a lot of virtual system administrators are less likely to be security experts. These individuals are often application engineers who work in a department such as finance and are tasked to start up, deploy and manage their own departmental virtual systems and applications. The flexibility of this kind of environment has a great many benefits to departments operations. Being able to start up and shut down computing power at will allows a computing environment that can deal with the changes of a department computing resource needs. This can introduce added data risk because of the proliferation of places data can run or be stored. It has the potential for operating in the shadows without the oversight of security staff or a department understanding and following defined security policies. This is also true when a department decides to use external cloud resources, which can be easily budgeted as a minor operational expense. A cloud connection to a department means it's also connected to the rest of their network systems. Whatever assigned purpose of the cloud to a department, the connection is now another avenue to stored organization data, potentially without the controls normally left within the purview of IT or security staff.

Can Education Be an Effective Patch?

Education is a continuous exercise in updating various user skills as well as bringing the uninitiated up to speed on security policies and procedures. Education, like systems patching, will always lag behind the level an organization actually requires of its staff. However, even with the best intent and the most rigorous effort to educate any staff, it can't keep up with changes in the computing environment or an organization's needs. In many cases, whether we like it or not, and whether saying this is politically correct or not, there is no patch for plain stupidity.[22] As an old saying goes, "The mother of stupidity is always pregnant."

With education, an organization can help make an uninformed or new staff member more knowledgeable and able to protect him- or her and the organization. However the ability to follow policies or simply exercise caution will be driven by the continuous work rush to do more than seems possible in a given period of time. This forces those who are simply not cognizant to the reality of how they can be duped, and who don't have the time or background to either spot or absorb crucial risk information, to greater exposure to making mistakes. This is different if it's a person who can never

---

[22] Wikipedia - Stupidity is a lack of intelligence, understanding, reason, wit or sense and may be innate, assumed or reactive.

understand versus ones in a constantly harried state, which is the norm for many. The ones who can't "get it" are black holes for security attentiveness and no matter what is poured into the abyss for security awareness they continually have high likelihood of being pulled over the edge of the singularity. There are plenty of people available for tipping into a black hole. And when some unsuspecting person does fall, it's often with little recognition of having fallen or the consequences of the dark pit they've introduced into their organization. The fact is that some people, no matter their intention, just don't and won't get how to minimize their exposure. These are not the insider threats that are a real concern—those who actively try to steal; most of the people who get sucked into this nightmare are just unfortunate bystanders to the threats around them.

We must be fair here to everyone. Is it appropriate to expect a person who has little to no computer expertise, and is just using it to do a job, to understand how it works and all of the intricacies of a system and its security? For example, most users of Facebook have no idea, or even care, what's makes it work. And why should they? Like most people, they use computers as tools, and don't necessarily need to know details of its operation. In fact most generally don't have time to find out. Most likely, a poor decision or action doesn't come from ill intent to expose critical data. Nonetheless, damage can be done, and someone will have to address the issues a person's actions generated.

The complexity or rules of society constantly change, with all the underlying systems that support a society so common to everyone that, over time, they are unseen. The unseen nature of computing means regardless of the individual or groups knowledge everyone is literally engaged with systems all the time. To expect everyone, or even a substantial number, to be able to be educated into awareness of all the systems around them, let alone the ones they use daily, is a dream about which security and IT folk must adjust expectations. Yes, there needs to be ongoing education. No, it won't stop innocent, ignorant, or simply stupid choices from being made, and that is where IT and security professionals earn their keep.

There is a simple but dangerous gap in some people's ability to connect critical points of their actions with any kind of risk. Yet we must acknowledge the complexity of computing today both in its underlying as well as visible arenas. When every member of a society is immersed with computing in everything they do, this just increases the size of every user's skill gap to the specifics of the computing environment. As mentioned earlier in this book, we really need to take a look at how to completely remove users as exposure points. Doing this would reduce attack surfaces substantially. The fact has been shown that this can't be done by education alone. It needs to be social engineering of security systems to protect the uninitiated, busy or anyone else from making mistakes. And it should do this without impacting the usability of their systems as they do their jobs, communicate or are entertained. There can be many means added to decrease risk, including more sophisticated but transparent access control and a security presence that is masked from users while protecting them. A focus would be for better immediacy in spotting and then mitigating issues at the user level before it penetrates an environment. Attackers rely on the fact users aren't experts and are busy, taking advantage of the constant volume and barrage of information and their need to complete tasks to get someone to make a mistake. These attacks are often well-engineered social exercises targeted at the inexpert audience who use computing systems to do their jobs. Of course, spear phishing can catch a trained expert as well. And there is a variety of other sophisticated attacks that can fool everyone from a computing- or security-challenged individual to security experts alike.

Stupid Is as Stupid Does

Carlo Maria Cipolla,[23] an economic historian, created five fundamental laws of stupidity that he called "The Basic Laws of Human Stupidity."

1. Always and inevitably, each of us underestimates the number of stupid individuals in circulation.
2. The probability that a given person is stupid is independent of any other characteristic possessed by that person.
3. A person is stupid if he or she causes damage to another person or group of people without experiencing personal gain or, even worse, causing damage to him- or herself in the process.
4. Non stupid people always underestimate the harmful potential of stupid people; they constantly forget that at any time, anywhere, and in any circumstance, dealing with or associating themselves with stupid individuals invariably constitutes a costly error.
5. A stupid person is the most dangerous type of person there is.

Without belaboring the point, we've all had our moments in the sun, both from the great things we've done in our lives to those moments that could be classified as mistakes. For most of us, we operate with reasonable intelligence, but the reality is that sometimes a distraction, such as children, spouses, jobs, or pressure, drives us to a moment we may regret; that is the normal state of being human. The difference is that a normal, intelligent person (who can be ignorant of many things) can figure out that he or she may have blown it. This can be even if, when it comes to a computing system, they weren't sure how they may have blown it, which is where education can help. The stupid ones don't

---

[23] Wikipedia - Stupidity

even notice or consider the possibility; thus, they are a danger to themselves and to the rest of us. One job of security should be to minimize the possibility of poor action and, if such an instance does take place, minimize the damage. Obviously, this is a tall order at which to succeed.

The Necessity of Patch Management

There is a constant stream of public announcements coming from technology companies regarding both bugs and vulnerabilities discovered in applications and systems. For instance, one estimate that circulates regarding the average number of bugs (some may create vulnerabilities) is ten to fifty bugs per thousand lines of code (per KLOC).[24] When you consider that Windows has about forty-nine million lines of code, based on the above formula that means it has tens of thousands of bugs. If these were fixed at the rate of five per week, it would take centuries to fix them all, and that is just one system. Interestingly, now we have to also include all those lines of code written by companies that aren't even considered to be software technology companies such as car makers, airplanes, home appliances, etc. These lend to the global body of billions of lines of code, thus millions of bugs and vulnerabilities, as ever more software code is embedded into almost everything made today.

According to a SANS Institute definition, "a patch is defined as a piece of software to fix problems with or update a computer program or its supporting data."[25] According to the National Institute of Standards and Technology (NIST) in a paper by Murugiah Souppaya and Karen Scarfone,[26] *patch management* "is the process for acquiring, installing, and verifying patches for products and systems."

---

[24] http://www.mayerdan.com/ruby/2012/11/11/bugs-per-line-of-code-ratio/

[25] SAN Institute Patch Management Policy 2009

[26] Guide to Enterprise Patch Management Technologies (Draft) Recommendations of the National Institute of Standards and Technology

Finally, according to a blog posted by Chief Banana, "a patch management policy needs to strike the balance between security (reducing organizations vulnerability as quickly as possible) and productivity (ensuring that upgrades don't disrupt business)."[27]

Patch management as discussed in a paper by Brad Ruppert[28] from SANS Institute states that patching is a routine process that should be as all-encompassing as possible to achieve the highest level of effectiveness. When we look at the facts that there are always weaknesses, vulnerabilities or bugs built into systems, having an aggressive methodology to better ensure that these are covered as quickly as possible is an important foundation for comprehensive security. The simple fact is that if known vulnerabilities aren't patched, it increases the attack surface that a hacker can use to penetrate an organizations network. For a productive patch management environment, an organization must create and communicate a comprehensive set of policies and procedures, ensuring written acceptance from all parties. This is because patching not only requires the efforts of system administrators, but also support from an entire organization. Patch management plays an important role in upholding good enterprise security posture but should not be treated as the solution for all security vulnerabilities. Patching is an absolute necessity. At the same time there are just too many systems, security designs, and implementation issues that need to be initially and continually addressed to ensure they're kept up to date and problems addressed.

Discovering areas that require patching, or vulnerabilities, can come from the code authors as well as others with an interest in finding and publicizing issues needing to be fixed. When we look at the tens

[27] How to set the best patch management policy Posted by Chief Banana on May 31, 2011 www.securitybananas.com as an excerpt from guest Gary Sims on behalf of GFI Software Ltd.
[28] Patch Management, part of standard operations Author Brad Ruppert 2007

of billions of lines of code deployed today, whether as software only or firmware in hardware systems, it seems reasonable to expect the rate of bugs or vulnerabilities and their discovery will continue to grow rapidly. When accounting for the continuous addition of more interconnected devices that rely on software, continuous and rigorous patching with a priority of most important first is critical.

A method of discovering vulnerabilities is through vulnerability-scanning software systems. These can be deployed for continuous scanning and discovery with recommendations to update or fix vulnerabilities. They can be set to alert IT based on the criticality of a system that needs a patch instituted. This ongoing process with network systems may require deploying an agent as well as checking devices and systems constantly, which has potential to impact system operation, traffic levels, and network processing power. Any impact must always be considered in this area to maintain user productivity. Based on the number of devices connected, the time it can take to scan each device, apply any necessary patch as well as notify IT and update databases means that no entire set of devices are ever up to date. Patching while integral to security is still a reactive exercise. At the same time, this information needs to be used as another input to understand the state of an environment and add to the knowledge base for security as yet another view into its overall protection status.

Having the ability to compare profiles of systems' and users' activities as per defined policies and usage patterns can aid security. This should be associated with ongoing activity of all entities and devices within a network, as they tend to have specific patterns of activity with other systems and applications during a normal day. Being able to note when abnormal activity may be taking place regarding a user or a system can be a preemptive means of identifying and addressing a potential issue. With user profile scanning, this can provide indicator activity regarding a person or a system that is acting out of normal operational parameters. It could be as simple as a person posting to job or trying to visit questionable external sites. These sites may not be blocked by a URL filtering policy, but it would be clear that staff shouldn't be accessing them from an organization's system.

For processes, methodologies, or activities that any organization needs to define, implement, and clarify, user profiles and system patch management must support the fundamental work responsibilities of individuals and the organization. Too often, organizations get caught up with their processes and methodologies as though they are strategies. First and foremost, the purpose is to create and support a trustworthy computing environment for users. This means a patch management/security ecosystem that supports system and data trustworthiness and data integrity as an overarching organizational strategic objective.

Organizations need to have a clear set of goals for a patch management/security ecosystem that can take into account the interwoven computing activities of users. This requires making patch management as integral to a security ecosystem design as possible to support organizational goals. Done comprehensively, it has to support key elements of any computing ecosystem: data confidentiality, integrity, and availability (CIA). If there isn't first an agreement on the foundational goals of patch management within a security context in order to meet CIA, it will likely be more difficult to design a patch management/security ecosystem to be effective. And if it isn't effective it's likely because the strength of systems security effectiveness is defined by its weakest link, which means that every link to security, including patch management, must be addressed equally.

Every organization's members produce tremendous amounts of data that they themselves, customers, partners, and suppliers rely on to conduct business. If there is a lack of trust in the data, it can impact the level or the possibility an organization has to succeed, essentially shackling its effectiveness and daily operations. There are many articles on what patch management does, how to do it, how to define processes, and what to protect. In reviewing many of these I didn't find one that described what the most crucial reason for an organization to operate patching effectively—trusted data and overall security. Data confidentiality, integrity, and availability are part of the foundation for a patch-management process, which also is a part of a robust security ecosystem. Even though there are a number of different standards that a variety of organization types may follow, such as industry, government, or military. The decisions about how it should work or what policies and priorities are defined as well as the selection of methodologies will impact the initial creation and continued support for a trusted computing environment.

Maintaining a trusted computing operating environment is another part in the requirement for intelligence and visibility. These are fundamental to secure a computing environment and all of its users, devices and data. One area that causes many companies difficulty is their ability to identify and prioritize all of their data, particularly their most important data. A key part of this is determining what applications create or utilize that data as well as the systems running all those applications and the staff members with access. In the process of identifying all of this information, regulatory and patching priority requirements need to be included. These can often impact specific data and may have rules that define the type and level of access, patching regimen required, and other areas impacting how that data may need to be prioritized.

A source of regulations in this area is in published standards by NIST.[29] This standard lays out requirements for certain types of

---

[29] NIST Special Publication (SP) 800-53

activities as well as a patching design to address organizations configuration management processes. There is also the NIST standard Security Content Automation Protocol (SCAP)[30] that is "a suite of specifications that standardize the format and nomenclature by which software flaw and security configuration information is communicated, both to machines and humans. SCAP can be used to maintain the security of enterprise systems, such as automatically verifying the installation of patches..."

According to a study conducted by the Computer Security Institute,[31] there has been a tremendous increase in the number of virtual servers; by 2014, they project that 74 percent[32] of server systems will be virtualized. The CSI study further states that only 24 percent of tools used today were designed for a virtual environment. The question becomes the following: If the tools for system and security management, such as patch management, are not kept up to date to manage new environments, can it foretell any level of effectiveness with an increasing number of virtual systems or the explosive growth of mobile BYOD devices? Again, what we see here is the proliferation of computing systems, whether server or endpoint types, along with the growth of security systems, which continues to complicate the world of securing systems and data. How can all of this be cobbled together within an environment that allows visibility, quick and thorough investigation, and the ability for deep analysis and response to issues spotted across the entire computing spectrum? Not one device at a time, as seems to be more of the case today.

---

[30] NIST Special Publication (SP) 800-26
[31] Computer Security Institute 2010/2011
[32] Gartner 2012

Chapter 7

What to Expect in the Future

A Little Background on the Process of Hacking

The actual process of hacking a target has many similarities between each separate incident—it has to start with a point of entry, which is normally an endpoint or a user-accessible device. So that entry must be found first, then any follow on activity can be based on what is found inside the penetrated organization. For instance exploiting vulnerabilities or bugs, a hacker will identify what applications a target organization may be using that they have usable vulnerability information about. Once penetrated, a hacker can begin the work necessary while inside a target to get the items of value wanted in the first place.

There will obviously be variation with initial entry, but a type of initial target will be pretty much the same—endpoints and a user or users. An entry can be an attempt at brute force, but it is more likely going to be some type of phishing attempts that are designed to lure a target to click on an attachment, a link in an e-mail, or something that can open the door for a malware download. Spear phishing occurs when the hacker has done research on his or her specific target—for example by researching the target using social media the hacker can learn a lot about them. This can include areas such as hobbies, preferences, attitudes and connections—assembling an attack that looks like a normal e-mail based on this background research to the target to get them to take the bait. There can be any number of attack styles based on the hacker and the target. The hack may be an active methodology, where the attacker continues to create situations with spear phishing to try and entice someone to compromise his or her environment. Once that is done, the hacker can then go into the next phase.

A hacker can also use more passive methodology to get in. For instance, they may seed an area with USB sticks containing malware that can self-execute when plugged into a computer. This can be set up to load malware from the stick and then make a call to an external system, a "call home" to get additional instructions for the next steps. The goal of course is for the hacker to gain control of that device and branch out from there. Unfortunately if someone foolishly picks up a stick and plugs it into a computer if it has malware the attack has begun. In vague targeting that dropping a USB sticks represent, the attackers hope that a viable target will pick up the stick, plug it in and any endpoint protection won't block installation from the USB. This is not a very viable methodology as there is little that an attacker can do to direct what happens with a stick. Different types of phishing and many other methods have proven to be workable and, unfortunately, a fairly reliable method as long as a hacker has patience. Most likely, a hacker is working on multiple targets and methods at one time and will go to the one that succeeds first.

Any initial penetration will be different based on a target and the hacker's intentions, whether it is stealing, disrupting an organization, or perhaps installing ransomware, which has tended to target individual users, but of late is clearly now targeting organizations as well. The process of an attack is far more than just the initial penetration of a target system. The process of an attack, for instance targeting a vulnerability or bug and attempting to exploit it, is generally a set of discreet steps. The hacker takes multiple smaller steps for any kind of attack such as an exploit because it makes it more difficult for defenses to spot their activities. It can also be a form of evasion by taking smaller steps and then removing any history or log of them as they move through the exploit process. Again this methodology is all about making it more difficult for defenses to detect an attack by various masking of the processes the attack puts in play.

If an attack is very obvious and visible to a target, it's likely a distributed denial of service (DDOS) type. These are intended to be visible and meant to overwhelm and disrupt an organization's computing environment for some period of time. Often, these are not necessarily meant to steal anything but just to make a statement by making a target network or web unavailable. This is quite different than spear phishing or stealth used to penetrate a target. In the case of stealth, if a target knew they were being attacked it would run counter to a hacker's intention and make it more difficult for the attack to succeed. In these areas, any way a hacker may inadvertently announce or show their presence would clearly go against the initial purpose for using a stealth approach. Either way, these activities can be damaging and disruptive in a number of ways. The latter stealth attack generally has more long-term consequences and a greater potential for substantial damage to any organization or individual. A well-executed stealth attack that attains its goals can create enough damage to an organization that can reverberate within the brand's image for years after it actually happened. As we know this can cost millions of dollars in lost revenue, jobs, and the resource demanding task of finding and cleaning up areas that allowed a penetration to happen in the first place.

In the initial phase of an attack, a perpetrator needs to work out a number of preliminary activities, such as identification of a target and information gathering on a target (or targets) that enable them to build attack profiles. The information a hacker can gather helps determine the best type of attack that looks most likely to succeed. Though, as one would expect, even hackers have preferences and styles they will default to regarding targets and attack methodologies. Often, the type of attack will remain the same one the hacker used successfully before. Also, different hacker groups will tend to have identifiable styles or techniques, along with a preference for particular tools that they have to use in their quiver. When one considers how much work it takes to build an attack from scratch each time, it makes a lot of sense that hackers would also try to reuse previous work. In a real sense, all of this information becomes a type of signature on not only a hacker or hacking group, but also as an identifier as to where the source of the attack likely came from. The list below covers some of the thinking that can go into the exercise and information hackers may want to gather in preparation for an attack.

Different organizations fit into different categories based on a set of common types of systems and ways that they conduct their business. Depending on the hacker or hacking group, the intended target may be determined by what the attacker already knows and their existing skill set. If the perpetrator is a hack for hire, it could be there management or a contract that specifies the specific industry or organization. Often, these fall into categories as mentioned above, such as retail, defense, financial, not-for-profit, and manufacturing. There are a lot of variations to all these, though there is enough commonality with organizations in the same business category that a successful attack on one organization in a category has an already proven element for attacks on others in that same category.

The type of business will determine the types of computing resources a hacker would expect to see used by organizations, including:

Retail (POS-type systems)
Manufacturing (SCADA or robotic-type systems)

Bank (ATM systems)
Financial (trading systems)
Consumer goods
Transportation systems (public and private)

Other questions include what kinds of other organizations a primary target company contracts with and would likely have network connection. For instance, a retail establishment may have set up electronic communication with many vendors that support them so that they can bill, pay on purchase orders, order product or services, or conduct a myriad of other activities. A perfect example of this is Target's relationship with an HVAC vendor that provided maintenance of their buildings' air-conditioning systems. It ended up that as a smaller organization they will tend to have far fewer threat protection skills or resources, was the avenue hackers used to get into their primary target's (pun intended) systems. Obviously, any external organization could perform many different services, such as janitorial, building maintenance, physical security, product suppliers, accounting or payroll, and banking. The main aspect is exposure can be through any vendors who provide any kind of service for a retailer where there is also some kind of electronic communication between the parties.

Another area attackers may be looking at is how dispersed an organization and their computing environments are, the number and type of facilities, and whether the facilities are spread out across a wide or limited geographic area in a few large or many smaller branch type facilities. Also, based on this information, assuming there are computing systems at all sites, one can surmise the number and skill level of cybersecurity or computing experts at any given site would be of interest to a hacker. What they could expect, is that smaller sites will not tend to have dedicated security personal, but they will be managed from a single or limited number of sites. Obviously attackers will target a company based on the information they want to obtain, that if a hacker attacks a retail organization they best not expect to get engineering drawings of a stealth fighter aircraft.

Other areas of consideration would be the level of expected sophistication an organization has regarding cyber protection. Where the skilled people are located as well as the logical and physical location of systems. For instance, if the company uses a cloud vendor for some or all of its computing, who is the vendor and what does that vendors' computing and security footprint look like? It's also important to consider the type of computing a company is doing with its cloud in combination with its other computing resources. It would be different if an organization is 100% cloud, or a combination of local data centers and cloud that creates a hybrid computing environment. Is the cloud used for the external web or is the company also operating more internal organizational systems and applications in cloud systems? This could include various office application suites, e-mail, and sales or financial systems used to run the various functions of their business.

Once a hacker has identified a viable candidate, the next step is to review methodologies for entry based on the specific organization, its type of business, and employee skill as well as types of jobs they may do. This will be included along with available information the perpetrator may have gathered on the organizations personnel and systems. A hacker may modify his or her attack based on the target, information they have gathered about it, and the available entry points, such as partners, vendors, or associations. Normally, the hacker will continue to follow his or her same style used in the past, particularly if it's proven to have had any success in previous hacking activities.

For a start, the perpetrator may build entry profiles appropriate to specific target business types; for instance, a method that could be used for retail organizations is to target their distributed POS as a primary source of valuable information once initial penetration has succeeded. The question becomes how to get to those systems without being spotted. There will likely be a different methodology for a manufacturing environment versus various types of financial organizations, such as banks or stock-trading companies, or a retail organization as discussed above.

What an expert hacker likely decides regarding an attack profile will be partially determined by the characteristics of the target as well as the hacker's capabilities. Also, as mentioned previously, every hacker has tendencies, preferences, and a style that doesn't vary that much between attacks as well as preferred target types based on what they may have succeeded at in the past.

Just like anything else, there are a lot of average-skill level hackers who utilize tried-and-true attack types and tools that are built by more expert hackers to conduct their work. Those with higher-level skills can elevate lower skilled hackers when using professional grade tools. The tool authors may take a percentage of the gain or simply sell the tool with a support contract. Either way, this enables less-skilled hackers to both increase their skills and to utilize higher-skilled hackers' knowledge and experience via better tools. Unfortunately this will make them a more formidable opponent, if for any other reason than forcing defenders to maintain certain types of defenses to keep the constant attacks out. That means the defenders have to painfully burn resources to keep the lower level hacking process under control, which may take away from protecting against more dangerous and skilled attackers.

How the entry took place may determine the next steps in the attack. A common effort will be for an attacker to elevate their access privilege status and gain more open access to various parts of a network environment. This makes it easier to cover their tracks as well as to identify key target information to take because they are seen as just another authorized user. It's pretty standard procedure to try to get the highest-level access to systems and data as possible. This makes it easier to map out key targets in a network, and conduct more detailed searching for the target information and high value systems. To get this going, it's important that hackers identify a key type of individual as well as specific individuals that either have the kinds of access they need or can be an avenue to getting it.

Also, a key part of the building process is to find individuals who are visible targets. This is much easier due to many social-media connections that allow easier tracing of business and personal connections and interests. Attackers can review different vectors for the attack so that they can have multiple points of entry and fallback points should their initial attempts fail. Even if the first attempts don't succeed, hackers don't stop but will continue to target the same individuals through spear phishing.

A target with a large number of identifiable internal/external professional and personal connections is a rich target indeed. This gives a hacker greater opportunity to spoof a communication from one, or many, of the targets' co-workers, acquaintances or associations. For example, the target could be a company recruiter, sales person, or anyone who tends to have a lot of unsolicited communication from unknown parties. The solicitation could be from parties who are, for instance, looking for a job, or want information on a product. This is a normal state with these types of professions and will lower the chance of hacker communication being seen as unusual. So in a target's normal course of business, they will expect to communicate with a wide array of unknown external parties. Because of that, they won't tend to question getting a contact from individuals or groups they're not familiar with. And they are also less likely to overly scrutinize the contact information either. Also, a target who is a joiner tends to like to belong to clubs, teams, and professional organizations or other social groups means the variables available for an attack communication is wide open.

Having information that is easily available on public sites (Linked-In, Facebook, etc.) allows a hacker to easily discover as well as connect to an individual via those sites. Though social sites attempt to protect users, the fact is that verification by most of these sites is not strong enough to deter reasonably capable hackers. These types of sites want to sign up as many people as they can and encourage communication, so they are compelled to keep the threshold for verifying identification of an individual easy enough that creating a false persona is not that tough to accomplish. The fact is that any materials that enable a hacker to build credible communications with a target, such as pictures, school or organizational logos, websites and pages, and references to other information, only add to their credibility. This makes it even more difficult for a target to identify the event for what it is and will normally assume it's a new communication, from someone they have a common association with to subsequently meet online.

The Hacking Process

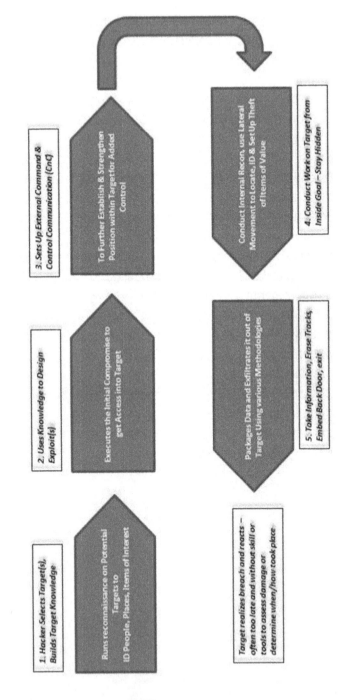

1. Hacker Selects Target(s), Builds Target Knowledge

Runs reconnaissance on Potential Targets to ID People, Places, Items of Interest

2. Uses Knowledge to Design Exploit(s)

Executes the Initial Compromise to get Access into Target

3. Sets Up External Command & Control Communication (CnC)

To Further Establish & Strengthen Position within Target for Added Control

Conduct Internal Recon, use Lateral Movement to Locate, ID & Set Up Theft of Items of Value

4. Conduct Work on Target from Inside Goal – Stay Hidden

Packages Data and Exfiltrates it out of Target Using various Methodologies

5. Take Information, Erase Tracks, Embed Back Door, exit

Target realizes breach and reacts – often too late and without skill or tools to assess damage or determine when/how took place

Sophisticated Players with Powerful Tools

There is a clear divide in capabilities between a majority of hackers and highly skilled professionals. I don't want to confuse the term "professional" with whether a person spends time doing something most of us feel is dishonorable; it's simply the capabilities they can apply to the time they spend within whatever work it is that they do that differentiates a professional from a nonprofessional. The less professional hacker is considered a script kitty, basically following instructions from the systems they have purchased from the skilled professional. Even if script kitty is someone who only has the skill to follow instructions or a formula, they still suck up defensive resources. A professional is a far more dangerous player, but at the same time, it would be foolish to make light of the script kitties. To be targeted by script kitties is certainly painful, but to be targeted by the professionals is daunting. It's simply difficult to protect against hackers who know not only the how and what, but also the why they're doing something a certain way. They have the focus to carry it out and already have a good idea of what the return on the effort will be before they even start. These people are very motivated and good. Script kiddies clearly succeed, but mainly by using cruder, more brute-force methods that tend to be repetitive, heavily relying on other professionals' tools. It doesn't mean they aren't a problem because the noise created by their constant pinging or attacks makes it more difficult to spot the more dangerous stealth activity. The skilled hackers benefit from the level of activity created by lower-level thieves, as they can help use all the script kitty noise to obfuscate activity they may be conducting. By hiding in the shadows of all the noise, it makes it more difficult for defenders to spot the activities of a more dangerous hacker within the constant din of script kitties.

Morons with Powerful Tools

The sad-but-true reality is that even a bad thief succeeds sometimes. We've all read the stories about the bank robber who hands a stick-up note to a teller that is written on the back of their deposit slip. Or the home burglar who, after finishing stacking his stolen goods in the middle of a living room, proceeds to have a meal, a couple of beers, and falls asleep on the couch. These are the thieves that cause minimal damage once in, due to their own incompetence, but the problem is that you can't really tell that they are incompetent until they get in. They can still get in regardless of their fundamental ineptitude. Because they can take advantage of the same tools for their attack as the sophisticated attacker, and with a bit of luck and a few hundred, or thousand, attempts, they're in and can then cause more problems than their lackluster initial attempts.

This means that any level of protection against any attacks, whether by a low or a highly skilled professional, should not be discounted. This should be similar to the strategy the city of New York started twenty years ago when they determined that even the low-level criminal act of jumping a subway turnstile could not be ignored. This was because they found it set the wrong tone to possible perpetrators. It turned out to be a very effective response that saw an overall lowering of the crime rate in the area. In the case of cybercrime, because any attack can be automated by running through an endless number of cycles at little actual cost to the hacker, they all have to be treated as seriously as the skilled hacker. That means there must be defenses designed to deal with each type. Part of a goal would be to force enough added effort spent on a hacker's part before they can succeed, hoping some may give up and go to where it's easier to get in.

As does everyone, hackers also have limited resources, so tying them up in one area means they likely have less time and fewer resources to spend in either perfecting their craft or going after more targets. Part of what a defender has to do, at minimum, is to make a hacker pay in time and effort greater than any little gain they may get from that target. The more time it takes any hacker, the better for the defenders. Even though a machine doesn't care how long the job takes, if attackers' time price for a visit to your kingdom is always high, unless the reward is clearly worth the effort, they will gravitate toward easier pickings. This is true for the efforts of lower-skilled hackers. However most likely it won't apply as much to nation-state activities, highly skilled hackers, or to ones who've been hired for a specific job. Whatever the case, a price needs to be forced on hackers in the form of more effort and time required for their success. This may help to increase the chance that they will redirect their energies someplace else.

Like the motive for bank robbery, the same is true today of cybercrime: There's money in it. Organizations can't change the value of the goods they hold with the hope that if a hacker thinks they have nothing of value, it will dissuade the perpetrator from targeting that organization. Thieves will go where they see value, cyber terrorists where they can create the most damage, and cyber espionage agents where they can steal the most important information. In any case, the smart ones will verify value is at a target before they spend their time going after any target. And value can be determined in many different ways; even something that may seem unimportant to a company may be a jewel to a thief.

Basic defenses can incorporate simple elements such as some evident means that indicate to attackers the need for them to dedicate more time to an attack, make it more difficult for them to evaluate the defenses in place or unable to calculate their risk in going after a particular target. The point is that an organization is in trouble if hackers believe they can deal with it with impunity. If a price for a hack is higher at one organization versus a similar organization with similar items of value, that alone can be a form of deterrent, at least for a while. Of course, that only applies if you're organization is sure it's the one with the better defense. Clearly, this would be a pretty crude means of self-protection. At the same time, hiding in a flock with others who are easier to steal from could be an acceptable form of defense, though I wouldn't rely on it for long. Obviously, it's just not good defense, particularly once a hacker has a specific preference for what you have.

Security-industry solutions tend to be very vertical in their capabilities, often due to the complexity of different types of threats that can be seen at different junctures within a network environment. Combining this and the variety of applications, systems, devices, geographies and other elements makes it difficult, if not impossible, to create a single solution that can address all security issues effectively. Many companies have tried, as we see in a number of companies offerings in products called unified threat managers (UTM), or a newer name alluded to as Next Generation (NG firewalls for instance). The design of these types of solutions attempt to incorporate a number of different security solutions in a manner that allows them operate together on a single hardware appliance. Unfortunately, the functionality of different security types means that neither hardware nor software can be optimized for any of these specific products. What tends to be delivered are systems that allow vendors to position the product as integrated together. The reality is significantly less than that as these systems may be on a single appliance and OS, but they can't derive intelligence from the flows between each application as they are still operating as silos, just on a shared platform. At best they can meet a good enough capability in their respective categories.

These systems all tend to run through their defined areas gathering information for assessment and analysis, generally not attending to traffic outside of their capabilities because these systems don't have an information-analysis sharing framework. For example, if you can only see half of a birthday cake, and there are ten candles on that half, many could reasonably assume the recipient is ten years old. However, there is also a high likelihood that this won't be true. The problem is that if someone believes their systems see the whole cake, confidence in the conclusion compared against actual data that drives a different conclusion in an assessment would create a wide swing in responsive action. Because there is no way of telling how right or wrong the assessment may be because only half of some unknown whole (the cake) can be assessed, the chances of a wrong assessment are high. And further compounding this kind of situation, the assessor won't have any idea how far off the mark their assessment may be in either direction. Consequently, many actions subsequently taken might be based on a picture of a situation that is thought to be correct, which of course will totally skew any assessment. In my estimation, the problem with trying to do everything in a single system, without intelligence sharing and actual integration between systems, means each solution has just a moment to take a look at the cake, and draw their conclusions. Some will see half a cake, some a quarter, some may see more. At issue is none of them necessarily knew what the others saw, so they have no comparative context to determine how accurate what they thought they observed may be.

Now with the level of computing and powerful software algorithms available, deriving reasonable conclusions based on massive data analysis turned into intelligence gives security better opportunity to protect against threats than even five years ago. However, it may be worse in the sense that it's easier and faster to come to a wrong conclusion, or miss any conclusion, because of securities specialized vision. As noted above, any one system can only ever see half, or less, of a cake. Security intelligence means being able to combine all those specialized visions and see as much of the cake as possible at once, from every possible angle.

Coming up with the wrong response quickly because of all our computing power is no better, and perhaps worse, than coming up with no response slowly. The former one may take wrong action or no action based on inaccurate observation; the latter is still waiting and watching for some clarity of the situation. Though not ideal, waiting is a better state to be in when data is incomplete or you're not sure what it may mean. In that state at least one understands what they know and don't know regarding a situation as it hasn't been disguised by a poorly considered response based on incomplete or inaccurate observation provided by a single specialized viewpoint.

According to the book *Race Against the Machine*,[33] the author cites an analysis that suggests that between 1988 and 2003, the effectiveness of computers increased forty-three m-fold. What's interesting is that better processor capabilities, according to this analysis, were a minor part of the improvement; the biggest was from more efficient algorithms. The capabilities of security have certainly benefited from this improvement in programming, but at the same time, so have threat capabilities.

Speaking of morons with powerful tools, the title isn't meant to denigrate the skill of people using a complex set of tools; obviously, they have to be intelligent to utilize any complex tool in such a way as to achieve their goal. However, like every profession, there are a lot more people at a mid-skill level than the skill required to be considered a master hacker—the ones who build effective tools that they use in their profession and also sell to others. This is more like gold miners during the California gold rush of the 1850s—some got rich, but, in fact, the largest group of people who made the most money were the merchants selling miners' supplies, not the miners themselves. The problem with hacking is that the tools are proving to be very good, giving a person with lower-level hacking skills or sophistication in their programming prowess the ability to create pretty effective attacks. And the tools allow them to be

---

[33] "Race Against the Machine" by Erik Brynjolfsson and Andres McAfee

persistent, to execute their attack over and over, adjusting it as needed. And this can take place until they either succeed or decide on some other target. Based on the processing power they may have, this continuous attack can go on for quite some time in the background of other ongoing nefarious activities.

There is little cost for hackers to continually run a computing program and system that is attempting to penetrate an organization. Obviously no one has endless computing resources; however, this is where having a botnet[34] helps. The situation in hacking is much like a dedicated fisherman; no matter whether you cast five hundred times, you're only looking for either one big fish for dinner or a couple of smaller fish as the equivalent of a big fish. The cost per cast isn't the issue, as the fisherman has time on their side. An experienced fisherman won't expect to catch something every time. And if he does catch something, examine it, and if it's not what he's looking for, he will throw it back and cast again or even use it as bait for a bigger fish. In the process, the fisherman knows he will lose weights, lures, and other components. In the case of hackers, their loss is time or getting discovered, which normally has no penalty but means they have to start over with that target or try a new one. There are many possibilities that can result from hacker's or fisherman's activities. Since both parties obviously prefer spending their time hacking or fishing, they're willing to wait out the time it takes to achieve the results they want. The actions for the hacker are the same as the fisherman—cast, reel in, cast, reel in, adjust, move down the beach if surf fishing, change lures, cast, reel in, cast, and so on.

The advantage and benefit hackers have is that they can actually go fishing, albeit spear phishing, with notifications when they get

---

[34] Wikipedia - Any number of Internet connected computers communicating with other similar machines in an effort to complete repetitive tasks and objectives usually used with a negative or malicious connotation.

a strike. Once in, hackers can select their next move based on how they got in, the type of target, and the way a target is hooked. For instance, did they get in through someone with high- or low-level access? How can they use it to advance their goal? This gets back to the reconnoitre step within a catch's environment, as discussed in the hacking process earlier in this chapter.

Chapter 8

Social Engineering Explained

According to Wikipedia, social engineering, in the context of information security, refers to psychological manipulation of people into performing actions or divulging confidential information. It's a type of confidence trick for the purpose of information gathering, fraud, or to gain system access and differs from a traditional con in that it is often one of many steps in a more complex fraud scheme.

The term "social engineering" as an act of psychological manipulation is associated with the social sciences, but its usage has caught on with computer and information security professionals, as it can be readily applied to security hacking or protection.[35]

Cons or conning people has existed throughout human history. This can include magic or trickery for fun all the way to the art of pickpocketing, brazen or stealthy robberies, or "legal theft" conducted within existing laws. Legal theft includes the old Tammany Hall political gangs in New York or the cyber gangs of today. Whether these are legal or not is partly due to the actor's home jurisdiction or whether the laws are specific enough to pertain to the perpetrators actions. In a number of countries, as long as they don't perpetrate their hacking on the local population, all is well. This can also include pyramid schemes, such as that executed over decades by Bernard Madoff,[36] resulting in billions of dollars in losses for his clients. This was socially engineered fraud. He is so notorious that there is an extensive Wikipedia

---

[35] Wikipedia
[36] Wikipedia Bernard Lawrence "Bernie" Madoff

entry on him and his scheme because of the long stretch of time it went on and the huge losses involved. His application of social engineering was designed to appeal to human trust and traits that often result in a person asking few questions of a perpetrator or ignoring any doubts they may have toward a person who looks to be very successful. Once some level of trust is established between perpetrator and victim the tendency for people are to be less likely to conduct a closer inspection or an objective review which in a normal situation would have aroused a victim's suspicion. Accepting that there is no free lunch, instead of hoping there is, would likely induce people to take a harder look at the reality of the returns promised. People simply had to put aside any doubt they may have to buy into the scheme in order for the perpetrator to carry it out.

Within complex societies that utilize massive amounts of technology, social engineering is in our everyday lives so much that most of it goes unnoticed. Luckily, most of it is also reasonably benign. Over time, people accept complex technology as an unseen part of their lives. They quickly fold new technologies in and subsume it into the white-noise technology fabric of daily surroundings. And as we've seen, new technology may slowly, or sometimes rapidly, change the way people conduct themselves within a variety of the activities. It basically can reengineer their social approach based on the demands the technology puts on a society, doing it one individual at a time. Regardless of how complex any technology is, when it has become an invisible web wrapped around our every activity, people no longer have the ability to escape its tendrils, even if one desires to do so. Most societies today would have serious difficulty surviving without the many capabilities utilized from hundreds of years of applying technologies. For example, many individuals may find themselves at a loss on how to socially interact without the devices they use today. What has happened with the incremental creep of technology is that most of society's members can no longer disassociate technology from their daily activities. Members of a society generally have a subliminal awareness of all the technology within their lives, but rarely do they question what is there, its purpose, use or even its suitability; it's just there.

Technology is now, at any level, not just a part of the fabric of our lives, but the fabric our lives are wrapped within, a cocoon of invisible pulses. If you were to attempt to peel all this technology away from humans, like trying to pull off the layers of an onion, you would find that the layers of technology are so thin and ordinary that they disappear between the layers of our lives. The fabric and our lives are so completely intertwined that pulling out what may seemingly be a single innocuous part could reverberate throughout the entire fabric and impact many lives. This fabric has many good points and a number of not-so-good points. The good points are the tremendous things we can do because of the prevailing technology; the not-so-good includes the tremendous damage we can do to each other and the world with that same technology.

Cyber hackers' use of social engineering is to take advantage of how humans conduct themselves inside this computing fabric as a part of their normal activity. A good cyber hacker understands that because everyone uses technology constantly, their awareness of any nuances in a specific session will be low. The intention of the social engineer is to slip inside of that window to be a normal part of a targets work or play motion so that the person doesn't quite notice anything unusual. A person just sees an event and clicks on it, like so many thousands of others that fall within their standard activity. For example, this event could be spear phishing based on research done on target individuals and a company that is made to look like a request from their HR department to update a personal file. The person who gets this likely opens it and goes through the process without much of a second thought. If existing systems don't detect the attack activity a user initiates, such as spotting a malware download or beginning of an exploit, the attacker has their first step in.

Historically, spamming was done using snail-mail flyers; the intent of an electronic spam is essentially the same. One difference is the frequency and cost to a sender to achieve a desired volume and thus results, the other is the time a target will actually take to evaluate and react, which in the digital world is much faster. And the limited time target parties take to evaluate something they received, within the volume they get of similar items, gives a significant advantage to the hacker. Obviously, the electronic type is far superior in all aspects because simple math says that the more you send out, the higher chance a person will click through. An example is e-mail that takes advantage of the majority of people who constantly "click through" their electronic communication, opening an email, attachments and links as a simple matter of course.

A hacker has to be as much a psychologist, anthropologist, and behavioral scientist as well as tech savvy to be really good at the trade. Luckily, the mix of skills required to be good are as daunting for hackers as it is for the rest of us. Unfortunately, there is a large enough cadre of supporting environments and tools built by good hackers readily and cheaply available to make even mediocre hackers a lot better. But even with good tools, mediocre will always be mediocre, unfortunately they usually aren't on their own. So when you have hackers as a group, their hacker social fabric and environment makes them individually better and also go after more targets at a lower cost. With group expertise, even if the individual isn't an expert, they significantly increase their chances of a hit, all while honing their skills.

Socially Engineered Security

Karl Popper, who was generally regarded as one of the greatest philosophers of science in the 20th century,[37] said that "piecemeal social engineering resembles physical engineering in regarding the ends as beyond the province of technology." To think that one can apply technology to a societal situation, either at the macro or micro level, to solve a complex problem, is similar in the vein to thinking you can build a bridge without considering all of the elements around the bridge, such as purpose, location, and the environment you want to put it in, which all impacts the end design. It is not just a mechanical exercise of assembling steel and cement at some haphazard location; it is a form of social engineering. This is because a bridge, like many other technologies, will change the way people travel and even interact. There are many bridges that created whole new communities, such as the Golden Gate Bridge in San Francisco. And a community is not just comprised of those living near and traveling the bridge, but also those who see it as an icon of a destination on its own, as its own ecosystem of followers of the bridge. People socially engineer their surroundings all the time using mechanical means. What is taking place now is a variation of this social engineering using digital means.

Threats are Socially Engineered, So Why Not Protection?

Popper also said, "We are social creatures to the inmost center of our being. The notion that one can begin anything at all from

ATTENTION: ENTERING
MANIPULATION ZONE

scratch, free from the past, or unindebted to others, could not conceivably be more wrong." This is the essence of the fabric discussed earlier. Security today, to a large extent, fails in a fundamental way because it hasn't taken enough into account that the

---

[37] Wikipedia Sir Karl Raimund Popper, an Austrian-British philosopher and professor at the London School of Economics

creatures it's dealing with are social by nature, as Popper states. The good hackers know this and take advantage of this fundamental flaw in both systems and security orientation. Security as a whole is not a technical answer. It needs to be socially engineered to be part of the computing community and the fabric of existence in which we live. It must be engineered in a way as to fit or be applied within social context of how a user absorbs actions into his or her life because they seem normal. Currently, security often forces user's to act as though it is a unique activity within the context of their computing. This forces users to have to consider and deal with security as a separate activity, which magnifies their experience of the complexity of their environment. To be effective, security needs to fit within the way individuals and groups conduct their work, public and private lives. This means it must be designed into people's work and their life orientation instead of being an innocuous set of required activities. Often these activities don't seem relevant to being secure against something such as a hacker that they don't actually see. A problem with this is the difficulty in making a connection between the act of computing use and how it may expose them. This is tough for anyone if they don't recognize the nature of threat actors and how all this security is relevant. It's easy to understand theoretically, everyone agrees there are threats. It's quite different to apply an awareness of threats when a user is flying within the wings of their digital experience.

Effective social engineering means that the authors of various protection systems must understand not only the technical environment that their solutions are being built for, but also crucially the social environment the systems will be utilized within. This includes how both individuals and groups will experience the "act" of being secure by using the technology. There are many products that are designed to be specific around a number of human aspects, from age to job role, and will reflect in their presentation and style of interaction the creators understanding of that audience. With security, designers don't have the benefit of being able to design for a single audience based on age or role, but to an audience that often has only a vague context of protecting themselves from computing bad guys. Obviously, as a product's purpose, that is laudable, but it simply isn't enough. The next generation of security products has to be a psychological fit and anthropomorphic in its insight into human-to-machine interaction, which would be giving a computing object more human characteristics. This is so that a user's role in a security ecosystem is so transparent that even a security neophyte (which is the majority) can adhere to it. That means they don't have to pass the gauntlet and struggle with the complexity that security usually presents. The burden must be moved onto systems that can enable user's security transparently for them. Unfortunately the current model will continue to present too many opportunities for failure.

What needs to be designed in security for it to be effective for users must fit into and reflect their computing outlook as well as their social expectations, all wrapped within a normal computing environment. This is not a simple task, and it will take combinations of experts figuring out how to best do this within a wide array of products. But like many products that were able to break new ground, they did so by incorporating their capabilities into people's experiential reality. This was done by realizing that a better way was to fit the experience of a device into how people normally experience and deal with their environment. This is instead of interrupting their normal experience for a moment of environmental assessment. The data exists today, and this approach exists in a number of non-security products as well, just look at your smart phone. Somehow, it needs to be assembled into cohesive solutions appropriately engineered for target users to fit into their work style and skill transparently. In conjunction, skilled security professionals must have continuous visibility, intelligence and management control of the entire dynamic user environment to ensure security effectiveness.

These solutions should not only secure its intended targets, but do so in a way that users won't fight them, which is too often the case now. They also should not need to pay much attention to it, and when they do it's not from the invasive notices we've all seen for so many years on areas such as changing passwords. For many users, as soon as something looks and acts like security, or something that the user "has" to do or "has" to follow, they often only grudgingly do the minimum necessary. This lack of attention and reluctant cooperation means the exercise is weaker because users often resist the security itself.

Human social interaction and expectations when utilizing computing, whatever it may comprise, is significantly different in one simple fact: Actions and results happen so fast, and feedback is almost completely masked within the environment. Computing security has been a bit of an outlier. There are a number of applications that do attempt to fit into people's lives, usually social media, but they miss the boat quite a bit when it comes to actually securing client information or even allowing clients access to manage their own.

Security or IT experts understand security systems' purpose, use, and fit it into their social fabric within the conduct of their jobs. But these are experts in the use of security technology. It's even difficult for them, as mentioned earlier, since there aren't enough of these people, and the systems and environment are so large and complex. To think that the masses of normal user just trying to do the job using a computer, needs to have any level of expertise in this area isn't realistic.

With ever more sophisticated hackers, the gap between those who know, those who we would like to know, and those who can't know how to be secure grows by the minute. To address this the computing environment needs to keep users from damage when screwing up. When a user screws up, a combination of software and staff needs fast notification to correct the problem and minimize damage. The point is systems must support what security personnel need to be effective, painlessly for all involved, except the hacker.

An example of employing simple social engineering in order to accomplish a task is the way a major airline loads its aircraft. The airline's focus was to create a social engineered process that could address a business need to load and unload aircraft quickly. It was set up in such a way as to involve customers such that they are willing participants in the logistics of loading the aircraft, essentially getting their passengers to self-regulate the boarding process. The process includes incentives, for instance the first to board can choose better seats. Also, those with early web sign up get a better position in line to board first along with awards for passengers who sign up sooner. Their frequent-flyer program also provides members with a better chance to get front-of-the-line privileges and earlier seat selection, all with the goal of enabling fast passenger load times. Of course, all airlines have frequent-flyer programs, but in this particular case, the award program is relatively generous, easy to make an award claim, so there is good sign up for the program thus their passenger loading ecosystem.

A goal of social engineering is to create cooperation between parties for mutual benefit. In this case, for boarding efficiency with minimal hassle for the airline, fewer staff and online departures. For customers a low cost in time system they can join to be able to be at the front of the line as well as gain free flights. Everyone wins.

TSA has created a similar environment with the TSA Pre pre-approval status through security. This is a self-regulating program that puts most of the effort on the individual wanting to avoid long security lines. Unfortunately for those of us who took early advantage of the benefit, the lines are getting longer because it works. At least in this case, most of those going through the TSA Pre line have a level of experience with airport security, so they don't tend to make the goofs many infrequent travelers make. Again, this is fundamentally social engineering, though it may be simpler than the airline, it took substantial thought and planning to execute. Perhaps it's not designing a security product and the experience a user would have with it, but fundamentally, it's about socially designing the user's experience in such a way as to encourage specific behavior. With security, a product must present clear benefit to users and encourage particular behavior. Besides security promising an esoteric state called "more secure" it needs to figure out how to achieve this "more secure" state so users will expend the effort commensurate with the reward. In this case, the primary effort should be user cooperation, and the reward is they don't have to think about or directly deal with security.

Chapter 9

Bringing Security Intelligence to Bear

As individuals or organizations, we all have to contend with the reality of hackers and the risk of network intrusion. A Chief Security Officer (CSO) at a major Fortune 100 company succinctly explained the overall dilemma of doing so successfully: "Hackers can get it wrong in 99 out of 100 attempts to penetrate a network, organizations have to get it right 100 out of 100 times to protect it." The sorry fact is that no organization can ever deliver 100 percent protection, no matter how good they may be or the tools and processes they use. There are too many elements and moving pieces—changes and players within and outside every computing environment that continually impact overall protection.

It is an unfortunate fact that it's impossible to deliver 100 percent protection against hacker penetration. Accepting this dim reality has to be considered within any protection strategy. This means what is done internally to discover and stop any attack is as important, if not more, than trying to block penetration. Continuous scrutiny via a combination of traditional edge-deployed technology and internally facing systems as information gathering would be used to populate a security knowledge base for constant consideration, correlation and intelligence development. Output could be quickly ranking various activities and events to allow analysts to focus on top suspects.

This is done where events or results are correlated within other activity to identify connections or traffic that may seem out of the ordinary for a multitude of reasons. It's crucial, with the limited time available, that analyst scrutinize the events that matter, not that are randomly picked from thousands of events hoping they've found those most critical to review. This means both cursory and comprehensive analysis capabilities must be available to build scenarios and what if queries dynamically and within an available knowledge base of intelligence. These can be used to help clarify what actually transpired, what it may imply, who could it or did it touch across network, devices, applications and users along with recommended actions combined into their knowledge base.

A knowledge base of intelligence is a source for conducting proactive forensic for historical and current identification and inspection. It could be a baseline in a number of areas, such as how your environment normally operates, including system, application and user communication along with standard traffic flow type and levels between all of them. This can be an ongoing exercise to conduct pre- and post-analysis on single or groups of events. A point is to understand both current state and how events or groups of events can compare to a historical threat state within various time frames. It can be used to help identify criteria to rank the chance of a threat state existing as associated with various network and device and other activities. All of this needs to be a continuous investigation of devices' and systems' current security footprint to see if it meets normal bounds or requires further investigation.

A posture of ongoing inspection and analysis can help develop greater sensitivity to an abnormal activity and trigger an investigation. Utilizing dynamic forensics to gather data for and characteristics of devices, traffic and the network as a whole can help create a forward leaning security posture. Instead of waiting to be breached, using areas of AI (Artificial Intelligence) such as Unsupervised Learning to constantly evaluate specific activity indicators as signs that can point to an external party inside the network.

There needs to be a combination of security AI and machine-learning in conjunction with human inspection, analysis and interaction. The intention of the machine-learning is to help remove superfluous traffic noise so analysts can focus on core information and issues. The machine-learning could utilize analysis algorithms on an environments traffic history, activity baselines along with comparative traffic patterns as some components in a filtering system. AI can be used to search for unknowns when you aren't clear on what the elements you're searching for may look like. And with modern threats there is always a human actor behind any attack, so there needs to be humans involved in any active defense. Once key events or incidents can be focused on by reducing the noise, humans with specialized tools can engage at higher level the events that deserve more in-depth investigation and analysis.

Building Intelligence Requires Visibility

So what is meant by visibility? From the aspect of what security staff needs to know about an environment they're managing, it means having the ability to inspect and analyze any aspect of a network, device, application, traffic flows, and users in every aspect possible, and quickly. The fundamental problem with this is that being able to see or capture every activity taking place within a network doesn't mean you isolate important activities crucial to protection. Modern networks and their devices, software, and user activities produce millions of events and incidents every day. Filtering out noise for an analyst to focus on those important areas is a necessary but complex and difficult task. Hackers will and do take advantage of all this activity to make it even more difficult for security personnel to spot their activities inside the noise.

Visibility comes down to a human analyst because software, as good as it may be, is only as good as its algorithms and policies ability to evaluate and isolate out activities. To be effective takes analysts and tools that enable in-depth investigation by security staff. A problem, of course, is that there aren't enough skilled staff members, which means that the tools must increase existing staff effectiveness. This means they must be able to customize and be quickly tuned by a staff member to look for specific information. There must also be available to apply threat intelligence that can help drive an analysts query capabilities to help dig into issues.

Hackers will run executables, need to communicate likely using encryption to protect their communications all while trying to stay out of sight. A hack is a procedural exercise, not a single point or isolated event but a series of related, though purposely obscured events or processes within a system. To determine a hack has or is taking place, an analyst needs to be able to identify and follow those trails quickly and effectively—utilizing intelligence baselines about systems, users, normal communications, and so on. The point of visibility means the analyst should be able to dig into any area of interest based on the need to follow a set of processes as noted above.

Chapter 10

Extracting Intelligence from Data

Building Intelligence and Threat Visualization

To address sophisticated and other threats organizations need to be able to tie their security systems information flow together, pulling from each to build an overall threat intelligence base. The base needs to also contain general and unique device, user and network behavioural characteristics, categorized by numerous elements such as destination and origin, whether it's known or new information and communication patterns and other characteristics. Including activity and status comparisons and correlated data feeds into the intelligence baseline can also increase its efficacy. This should help security professionals be able to assemble "knowledge chains" of events—activities that they can use to continually look for an array of indicators that individual security systems don't often note on their own. The need is for visibility, not just data access, to derive potential significance associated with multiple security systems output, activities, or items of interest being identified and collectively analysed. Often, events don't raise flags within a capturing system such as IDS, FW, or other security device because they can't connect that event to a wide variety of other events that may be related but are outside of their analysis scope. Bringing all these systems' knowledge together can create an association of data resulting in dynamic intelligence and analysis. This can help enable threat visualization by linking together superficially divergent information. This could be a step in the process of building a knowledge base of a network environment, users, activities and traffic flow.

Like the example company referred to in Frost and Sullivan's research with eighty-five different security tools from forty-five different vendors, this amalgamation creates its own set of problems and pretty much guarantees that all the diverse data can conflict and confuse any results an analyst tries to derive. Unfortunately, when one looks at the cost of the systems and overhead to run them, all that does is ensure that the value delivered is less than the money spent. Even if in the unlikely event the products are all from the same company, they would generally not share knowledge, classify threats in the same way, have similar user Interfaces, send their data to a single manager or even all be available on a single console. And these systems generally can't provide insight into a threat or event if the event is out of context of that systems design, and thus they treat those events as just more noise.

Intelligence, Intelligence, Intelligence
Threat intelligence needs to be pulled out of all the various security systems, agents, and management systems to enable correlated big-data security analysis on it. It gets back to digitizing existing labor, which, in this case, is data extraction, manipulation, and in-depth analysis for security and IT professionals to access a broad and rich security window into all network, user, application and device activities and imputed meaning to those activities. The goal is to exhume intelligence from all the debris that narrowly focused systems tend to ignore. Too much important data is lost because individual systems can't understand its significance. This impinges on speed of analysis along with efficacy and response time, because systems subject analysts to have to sift through irrelevant data. This makes it difficult to determine a current digital threat picture because an analyst can't capitalize on the gems of information that's hidden, not noted or simply misunderstood by individual systems.

Data can reveal hidden value by being subjected to an association of relationships that may exist between data flows, systems, and devices. Even a small-sized network environment with ten firewalls, a couple of intrusion detection/intrusion protection systems, a URL filtering gateway, antivirus software on every system, encryption, numerous other security devices, software application servers, and other systems generates enough events to bury analysts in its output. Add to the mix a few hundred users with multiple agents on each of their systems and a few dozen dedicated servers running twenty or thirty unique applications will easily generate millions of events every day. This environment requires constant updating and refreshing of signature files, ongoing policy tweaks, product additions as well as refreshing hardware and software. The noise of security and other devices, spitting out tens of thousands of logs and events that may need some form of cursory analyst review from numerous consoles, demonstrates the fundamental problem. There is no lack of data, but it's not treated within an interrelated sphere of data when coming from all these systems, security, or otherwise. This means only minimal intelligence regarding overall system traffic can be derived, leaving a lot of intelligence gaps that can, and are, exploited.

Security and other data must be turned into intelligence. To do this, it must be correlated across every system and flow so that all of the divergent bodies of information can become, ideally, informative points of view. These views can then be used to spot and drill down into issues quickly; serially, or in parallel. The purpose is to expose value from individual, seemingly unimportant events, which, at first glance, may not seem to mean much. But when making a comparison to other events noted by different systems, such as a SIEM, URL filtering software, or endpoint AV connections, observations of related unusual events can be discovered. This could take an obscure event that seems unimportant alone, but, when correlated to other innocuous events, exhibits something of concern. Intelligence is being able to pull all of these divergent activities and events together to identify these series of interrelated activities. Doing this should allow analysts to better identify threat indicators to drive their investigation into discovering inappropriate network or device actions. This can be as simple as detecting unauthorized access, a peculiar transfer of a sensitive file or other potential threat activity that individual systems didn't note.

Building Security Intelligence

The way that historic business intelligence systems can gather and analyze information from a wide range of sources is a similar orientation that a security intelligence system could use as a model. This could help address the need to interconnect the output of every security system and device and to excavate their output and identify areas of compromise, either active or potential, for further investigation and response. The feeds from all these systems should populate an intelligence-gathering-and-analysis system that can help evaluate and correlate all that activity. The purpose would be to give the analyst the ability to assess all activity and what that activity may imply as to a threat risk, along with a recommended set of actions, such as severing a current link, containing a device for further investigation, tracing out specific activity or killing processes. It should support gathering event information from agents on endpoints and servers as well as various applications activity and conduct levels of analysis via machine and human processing. Focused analysis by a professional should help pinpoint elements that indicate issues and be able to notify or stop and remediate a situation as needed.

Security intelligence needs to have the ability to analyze large database repositories for all activity that can impact security. It also must be able to provide a means to visualize results, utilize deep AI analysis to provide multiple angles that analysts can use to view and better determine their implications and whether additional queries are required. This must also address the need to customize analysis activities so they can address specific characteristics unique to an organization. Any security intelligence platform needs to provide security staff the ability to define high-level key metrics in one place and populate those across its environment. As well, being able to repurpose and tune policies and rules to support a baseline environment, while being able to alter each of them as a situation may require. Having more common security information sharing between systems, applications and devices helps to close gaps in security and create a more consistent information base to compare current activity amongst all the systems. Also, that would make it easier to identify a new gap and be able to correct it across the board versus system by system. This would, in essence, become a single-security intelligence system as the master for understanding all network, application, and device activity. The result ought to be a cohesive system that extracts and presents relevant meaning to all the output currently spewing from the mass of divergent systems deployed as a part of most company's security environment.

Intelligence from Machine Learning

According to Wikipedia, machine learning is a scientific discipline exploring the construction and study of algorithms that can learn from data and data flows. Machine learning, a form of artificial intelligence, can learn and acquire knowledge and become skilled at responding to situations by being able to assess large bodies of data. Such algorithms operate by building models based on constant input from a set of allocated resources and use that input to make predictions or decisions, (predictive data analytics). The difference is traditional programming follows explicit programmed instructions, which is the way a normal computer program or application functions. The fact is that though machine learning is far more sophisticated combination of instructions, it's still restricted by its fundamental programming, though significantly less.

A machine learning application could monitor network, devices, applications and normal user activity. It would use that information to establish what the environment generally would find to be a normal level and type of activity, communication and so on. Then, once essentially mapped out, the system could continue to monitor and learn from all of the activity and if something seemed out of the normal course of activity take some kind of action. This action could be alerting an administrator with information about what's being seen, what it might mean, and potential courses of action based on existing policies for dealing with any particular activity.

Machine learning can be considered a subfield of computer science and statistics. Its strong ties to artificial intelligence and mathematical optimization help it to deliver methods, theory, and application improvements based on applying their expertise for the machine-learning field. Machine learning is employed in a range of computing tasks, where the designing and programming of explicit, rule-based algorithms isn't feasible. Some examples of machine-learning applications include spam filtering, optical character recognition (OCR), and search-engine and computer-vision systems. Machine learning is sometimes confused with data mining, which is more of a method for extracting what may seem to be hidden data from existing data stores, which of course can have application to security. Machine learning is more similar to pattern recognition and can be viewed as two facets of the same field.

Arthur Samuel is considered to be the founder of machine learning. This is based on his initial work to create a checkers-based computer-learning program in the 1950s and his additional research around machine leaning throughout his career. Despite the relative simplicity of checkers, it still requires a level of strategy to play. Samuel thought that using a structured game like checkers could be fruitful in developing tactics appropriate to the general problem of creating a system that can learn from a structured activity. The main driver of the machine-learning structure is a search tree, with an example of a game search tree that he used below for tic-tac-toe. What he wanted to do was get his program to be able to cover all the variations in board positions potentially reachable from a current state. Below is an example of an abridged search tree to provide a simple visualization of how the process can work.

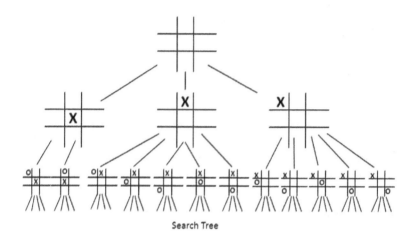

Search Tree

Because of a very limited amount of available computer memory at the time, Samuel was able to design and implement other techniques that helped minimize the amount of compute cycles needed for the game. One of many he came up with was instead of searching each potential path until it derived a conclusion; he was able to develop a scoring function that could be used to determine the next move based on a current position on the board at any given time. This function attempted to measure the chance of winning for each side at a current given position and took into account such things as the number of pieces on each side, along with the overall proximity of pieces as well as those in a position to being "kinged". He also used choices for selected piece movement for subsequent moves based on a minimax[38] (a decision-theory concept) strategy. This is where the system made a move that tried to optimize the value of this function, assuming that the opponent

---

[38] Wikipedia "Minimax"

was trying to optimize the value of the same function from his or her point of view.[39]

The same, but obviously more sophisticated and complex, aspect of machine learning is in use today in many areas such as security. It has value as an additive or supplemental technology. In its current state, it still isn't able to replace human investigation, analysis, and responsiveness as it pertains to more complex aspects of securing systems and data. The important part of machine learning capabilities is how it can help contend with issues that end up wasting hours or days of security analysts' time. Being able to reduce their time to understanding an issue can clearly provide benefit, but still, for the foreseeable future, as mentioned machine learning won't be replacing human involvement.

Visibility for Action

A security ecosystem that can extract data from various systems and apply analytics and machine learning to that data needs to also provide various ways for analysts to visualize all of the combinations it can present. This would cover the status of systems as well as applications, data, and devices. It also needs to be able to dynamically model suspicious activity or a potential security compromise as well as risk and other factors from the various data feeds. Utilizing methods that can uniquely portray existing or potential relationships between systems as they may relate to suspicious activity between them can help reduce discovery time. If analysts can quickly and clearly model different security scenarios, it can create an environment that is more robust and dynamically capable in determining an issue and assembling a response.

---

[39] Wikipedia "Machine Learning"

A benefit would be to allow IT security to derive quick pictures of particular activities along with the ability to drill down into specific events to identify sources and targets of the traffic. Having the ability to identify or link possible relationships between activities on various devices, and to do this while they're active, would be a form of dynamic forward leaning forensic intelligence. This could also tie in with industry events to see whether there were similarities between what an organization was experiencing and seeing in their environment, that may be unique to their industry. This could help them to be more proactive in hunting for activity associated with a rumored threat, even though they may not have noted any specific activity regarding the threat in their own environment at that time. All this can be brought together to potentially preempt a penetration as well as spot and block an active internal threat that was otherwise unseen. Visibility based on robust searching capabilities improve threat comprehension thus decision making regarding a need or type of action that may be appropriate. It can also provide a testing ground by modeling any different types of responses and their potential ramifications before live execution. During the process, a compromised system could be contained in such a way that could be undetectable to an attacker yet keeps an infection from spreading. This could be utilizing some form of a sandbox environment that can be invoked on an endpoint to allow seemingly continuous operation that an attacker would not be able to discern. The importance of this as part of the analysis is to have time to gain understanding of an attacker, their style and intent, and give an analyst the time needed, without threat, to ensure their investigation can be completed.

Chapter 11

The Knowledge Chain

Turning Data into Usable Intelligence

Methodologies for dealing with data protection throughout its lifecycle need to be significantly improved, regardless of data location, state, or origin of a transaction. In an earlier example about a retail business with thousands of POS terminals, dealing with the data for maximum protection means it must be enforced from the first point of its existence, such as during a credit card scan, and at every point in any transaction throughout its life cycle, essentially, forever. Ensuring that data is encrypted upon its creation and throughout all of its passages and storage can certainly increase its safety, but keys to decrypt the data can still be stolen. If encrypted data is lost in a hack, one can be fairly confident it can't be decrypted, but it can still expose an organization to some ugly issues. A positive step certainly is encryption, with additional steps for having security for any keys structured so that confidence in their protection is deserved as well as a backup plan if for some reason keys are compromised.

The true beginning of any primary data used during transactions is an individual's identity. The information required to ensure identity is such that if someone had it, he or she could use it for their own trusted transactions and benefit to the detriment of the true individual owner. Other data, such as a company's intellectual property, needs to be owned by the respective originator of the data or knowledge. In the case of personal identity and personal information, it's the individuals. In the case of an organization, it would be its crucial business data that identities and establishes it as a company. In essence, with a company, what it does is what it is, so all the elements involved with that process need to be owned by the organization. There are many opinions regarding data privacy and ownership for individuals, but the fact is that transactions all begin with and are based on identity. Any other data created stems out of simple but extremely valuable identity. Unfortunately, many of the methods organizations use for dealing with this core individual data does not support CIA (confidentiality, integrity, and availability) well enough, as most breaches attest to.

As noted earlier, there are tens of thousands of databases with information about each individual and organization, and have some means of identity verification. These systems are built and run by thousands of organizations, with the information stored within their own and remote or cloud storage. In most cases, even within a single system, they can contain conflicting and inaccurate information on an individual or organization all mixed together with the accurate information. The taint of questionable information essentially weakens any ability to ascertain individual identity as well as apply methods for verification of that entity. The difficulty in verification causes fundamental problems in any exercise to protect data and, in some way, impacts every transaction and every organization that relies on the vast stores of suspect data.

In India, Estonia, and a few other countries, there are federated or integrated types of systems (I use these terms interchangeably) to ensure a person's identity and make it very straightforward to verify an individual. In each of those countries it's also used by organizations and government as a part of their normal interactions with their citizens. The system in Estonia provides individual ownership of personal identity so any individual can warrant who he or she is, and ensure their information is kept up to date. This delivers a very high level of integrity, so the government can confidently allow the individual to access a wide array of activities as well as public and private services.

India has similar benefits, particularly when it comes to providing financial help. The financial help with India in the past was a system that provided direct food subsidies through a variety of channels. It was so difficult to manage that it provided a tremendous opportunity for graft, which was, unfortunately, widely taken. Now, any individual who has gone through the biometric identity process automatically gets a bank account where their allowance can be paid directly into it. Instead of a food subsidy system that was all too easy to corrupt, this system takes the middleman completely out of the picture and directly funds the verified individuals. All this is based on being able to first ensure identity and then warrant the individual ownership of that identifying information. This allows for use of the person's identity in a wide array of situations by ensuring the individuals identity could not be absconded or corrupted.

Chapter 12

Building Security from a Trusted Baseline

D ictionary.com[40] has a number of definitions for identity, such as the "state or fact of remaining the same one or ones; the condition of being oneself or itself, or a condition or character as to who a person or what a thing is and the state or fact of being the same one as (originally or currently) described."

Trusted Identities Are Security Management

A significant issue with identity is expecting that weak methodology can ensure the above principle of human interaction in a digital world; that is that people are who they say they are and remain who they purport to be. How much certainty can any organization have of an identity without a universal, accepted methodology of verification and a system based on multiple correlation points for an individual or company as an entity? The patchwork means of doing this today, with tens of thousands of records for every person and organization, has little means to be able to tell whether an individual or entity hasn't been usurped by another. This is because one means or place, even vaunted credit-reporting organizations in the United States can't absolutely verify that a person is who they say they are and the information a system contains is 100-percent accurate about the individual. Even some form of online identity verification with an IP address isn't reliable because the rigor to ensure who is at the other end doesn't currently exist. Much online activity can be spoofed well enough to fool many systems and individuals. The level of verification to be able to absolutely confirm

---

40 Dictionary.com - Identity

identity has limited legitimacy because the roots of most of the current validation capabilities aren't based on the irrevocability of an individual's identity. Unfortunately, it's all over the map. How can anyone be sure of any information they get from any system or person, particularly since there isn't an incorruptible methodology to prove systems, individuals, and entities are who they say they are? This means there needs to be a lot of inherent trust across individuals, organizations, and systems to allow the levels of various types of exchange taking place today to function; unfortunately, that trust is broken often enough to cause serious issue for those who don't have the means at hand to confidently ascertain whether someone or something is worthy of their trust.

How can we, as individuals or communities, be a part of an ecosystem that we can invest our confidence in the trustworthiness of its digital authority? Assurance in the subsequent verification of identity that can ensure an entity being engaged has been vetted (with ongoing verification) can warrant confidence in the overall transaction to deliver the desired results. The fact is that a lot of activity is conducted today in the digital world without any level of two-way verifiable trust between parties. Sure, there is SSL to ensure the data-exchange process is safe through an encrypted communication, but that may simply mean that a process is taking place by false parties or one false party and a duped party. Communication may be safe, but like doing the wrong thing at the speed of digital transactions, conducting a secure exchange with a bad actor just ends up with a bad result more quickly for the victim in the exchange. The risk to parties is still the same. Until one can explicitly trust the other party, the exposure to individuals and organizations in digital transactions still has unnecessary risk.

In the United States, what exists today is really just an ad-hoc digital identity and information infrastructure matrixed between multitudes of sometimes competing unrelated players. And each one has globules of unrelated but associated information on all the various participants. When taking all the potential participants and the infinite number of systems, entities, and sites for storage of identity into account, the chance of manipulation by a single party to its benefit echoes throughout the entire system. The fact is this is a mountain of information no one has a complete or even partial grasp of, increasing the risk to everyone with unforeseen consequences along with less than desirable transaction results. The consequence is unnecessary exposure of both good and bad data that influence a transaction in any number of ways. A more central ability to manage and protect personal information based on a higher trust value of the individuals and entities could help eliminate the high level of security and transaction expenditures being seen today. It would also help reduce data conflict, particularly as it pertains to the need for trust from various parties. This could also help to eliminate inaccurate or out of date information that just adds to the overall confusion. Without this, the fragmentation of identity and data, and the multiple places any one piece of identity and data can be located, will continue to benefit hackers. It's very simple to see that this scattershot approach provides hackers with many more avenues to practice their trade because it exponentially increases the accessible threat surface of identity and other valuable data that is the foundation for authentic digital transactions.

A federated identity system could help by providing trusted information to organizations and individuals necessary to transact business. This could make it easier to ensure that the systems where this information would be available to the market are rigorously vetted and can be trusted at the highest level. A federated system could be an identity-verification middleman, supported by industry, business, government, and financial institutions alike, without one having precedence over another. The savings for organizations would be more efficient spending on security to protect their internal IP, without having the constant issue of protecting information not necessarily germane to their actual business. This could mean more reliable and trustworthy identity-transaction data could be available from a single authorized and trusted source, instead of haphazardly scattered across thousands of organizations and tens of thousands data storage systems.

To enable the verification and trust needed regarding individual identity, a single, federated database system could be run by a third party, preferably a non-profit or government agency that would provide access service to organizations and individuals. It could be funded by initial membership and small transaction fees as well by government grant with an appropriate tax status. Its only goal would be to ensure that the CIA, confidentiality, integrity and availability of a person's or entity's personal identification information is met.

Don't Confuse Data Used for Identity Management as Big Data

There has been constant pushback from data-gathering industries such as Google and Facebook (though realistically, everyone is a data gatherer today) saying they need to capture and manage information (and note that this information often makes up an individual's identity) for their business. Without any intention by most companies to harm users, the companies claim having this information primary purpose is to allow a number of activities. Obviously this can be for conducting a transaction, improving their products, mining the captured information for market knowledge that can be used to better understand their demographic or target markets. It can also be assembled together in different forms and sold to others, or used to price existing services to a client based on the data's association to a particular client. It seems many organizations think that a part of big data is specifically an individual's identity, thus making identity management fall within their purview. Out of this also grows their need, or desire for financial purposes, to know every individual's personal identifying details, along with all of the marketing-related information associated with that person. In fact, identity management is its own element and not necessarily required for big-data analysis. Truthfully, big data is a methodology or means of processing large bodies of dynamic information, and, with the power and volume available for analysis, individual identity actually plays a very small part. Along with it playing a small part, based on all that volume, companies can surmise the who, what, where, how much, preferences and so on without having to also store personally identifying information about an individual. In fact, having personal identity information has very small benefit to a company but comes with a large risk to the individual and the company as well.

What is happening when every company tries to act as its own repository for sensitive personal identity data is that it puts information at greater risk of being exposed. As noted before, the many avenues to identity data increases its attack surface. In the big-data world, there is not much intrinsic benefit in knowing exact individual identity information except for a transaction and that can be achieved with far less risk to identity. And if that is needed for some other purpose, without exposing identities, there are enough means at hand for an organization to reliably figure that out.

The fact is that there is so much data these companies have and can get; they can easily correlate customer data to extract more relevant detailed knowledge about individuals. The information is there for them to understand individuals, groups, be able to identify categories of activity, and react to the players within that area by tuning their messages based on past activity, not necessarily exact identity. In fact, exact identity is mainly relevant for actually conducting a transaction. Volumes of data provide the ability to recognize patterns based on statistical exercises of the data, with the available depth and volume of data allowing a company to achieve very good predictive results for both individuals and groups. Not having companies store specific aspects of an individual's identity doesn't mean they wouldn't have their e-mail address, which would be up to the individual. As a part of the benefit of establishing core identity that has been verified is that individual is now able to have an e-mail or other address that is vetted and certified.

Big-data companies don't need to know every individual identity in detail for them to make informed business and marketing decisions. Identity details should be left to the act of conducting an actual transaction that is trusted because it has already been verified prior to its execution. It should also be a short-lived and transitory interchange so it can be ensured as a trusted process. The bottom line is that identity, once established, is essentially static information, whereas big data is a continuous dynamic feed of information and information analysis. All these companies need to know in an actual transaction is that the person, as noted earlier, is who he or she says he or she is, and the system confirms that. Once identity is established, it only requires keeping essential but fairly simple information updated, with its primary value of assuring a trusted transaction. Being able to assess masses of transactions, market data information on individuals and groups as well as other elements doesn't require the details of identity to have value and use for marketing and other purposes. An organization can still market or assess a 35 year old male individual living within a zip code with particular likes and dislikes without needing personal identification data on them.

If there is an effort to centralize personal information, it will require structural and conceptual changes in dealing with it and would need to support organizations' ongoing business needs through these changes. A first step, as a federated system is a longer-term solution, is for organizations to improve their security posture in dealing with data in the first place. Just ask Target, JP Morgan, Home Depot, and others what their exposure would have been if they didn't need to store any personally identifying information. Also, there are remedies that can help every transaction, data, or number used, if data is in an encrypted communication (as credit cards with chips are able to do) from the moment it's entered into a system and during any part of a subsequent transaction process. If an organization doesn't hold personal information in the manner it does today, along with encrypting each transaction, regardless of what happens from the point of purchase to the point of their payment by a bank, the potential for exposure would be significantly lower. Having personal information as well as credit card numbers stored together with a person's identity means that all this information is immediately usable. Including a lot of information about a person beyond the minimal necessary, as most organizations do, makes a great single repository for a hacker to target.

It seems unrealistic to expect that every organization will have the kind of security that can ensure all of the data they store is safe. It's frankly too much to expect. So if identity is to be truly protected, it needs to change to a system that can be managed within a single entity so that at least minimal levels of protection are in place. It can't continue to be a variety of ad-hoc systems run by tens of thousands of organizations with huge variance in their security approach and capabilities, even with the best of intentions.

Hackers and bungling fraudsters extract money from credit card and other credit mediums through identity theft. A problem the IRS continues to have in this area is a great example of identity theft and the mix of systems that make this a rampant malady. With the IRS, there are a number of laws, along with poor identity-verification infrastructure, that cripple its ability to protect against identity theft. The estimate of IRS fraud is in the billions. This is partly because of time restrictions they have in sending a return to the filer doesn't provide them time to verify a tax filer identity. Even if they had time to verify an identity, what system could they access and be confident of 100-percent accuracy in verifying a filer. A good example of how rampant this is occurred in 2012, when the IRS gave 1.2 million taxpayers special codes to file their returns because they were victims of identity theft. This was needed because all of them had false tax returns filed under their names.

Using security chips and getting rid of the magnetic security strip on credit cards is a good start to protecting transactions. A more robust environment can have elements such as dual-factor *authentication*[41] and be implemented via a centralized federated identity verification system. It could also make use of an identity card with a chip using some type of biometric verification versus today's sloppy methods. I understand a lot of individuals and organizations have concern over "big brother" having all of this information about individuals. In fact, there is a huge amount of data on everyone already that any "big brother" could use. Safeguarding it would be easier in a defined manner with rigorous governance of the data. If done correctly, the point is that the individual would have his or her information in their own control, not left to the winds of chance within thousands of unknown organizations as it is today. This should enable a single place for any individual to challenge information or update it, ensuring there are appropriate controls for this to eliminate fraud by an individual regarding their own data accuracy. This could create a more robust, trusted, and accurate system for everyone—businesses and individuals alike.

---

[41] Wiki - provides identification of users by means of the combination of two different components. These components may be something that the user knows, something that the user possesses or something that is inseparable from the user.

Two Models for Identity Management: Federated and Integrated

According to Wikipedia,[42] identity management basically amounts to a system with a common set of policies, practices, and protocols in place to manage the identity and trust of users and devices across organizations. There isn't a more complete Wiki definition on either federated or integrated identity management at this juncture. In the book *Digital Identity Management,* there is a chapter on authentication in business,[43] in which the author John Skipper differentiates between these two aspects of identity management in that federated is what he calls an issuer-centric model and a closed system. The author also states that the federated model is best suited to small communities with rich and intensive interactions and simpler risk management requirements. The federated issuer is also in it to make money. It seems reasonable that the foundation of a federated structure can determine any revenue goals and benefits they wish, such as Estonia as a not-for-profit ID system serving a specific community, the Estonian citizenry. It has very small risk due to the fact that the majority of the participants in the system are all citizens of Estonia with similar overall orientation and country goals. This means that the members of the community are known factors with a vested interest in the success of their country and their identity-management system.

According to the author, he describes the integrated model as application-centric. Skipper points out that an integrated model's application-centric focus is around a core set of trusting parties, rather than issuer-centric. And the integrated identity model orientation leans towards a community being a business or, as Skipper mentions, set up to apply to a specific scenario. This implies that a community may be limited to those primarily interested in

---

[42] Wiki - Federated Identity Management
[43] Authentication on Business by John Skipper

participating, with a common bond being the application, such as Amazon, Facebook or other types of communities. This could be a system that is set up to work for specific business purposes to ensure that all those who benefit from the exercise of online digital activity can equally certify the identity of all parties. There may be common needs across other application communities, such as banking. For instance a banking clearing system such as the global Society for Worldwide Interbank Financial Telecommunications (SWIFT) financial platform, a cooperative owned by 3,000 financial institutions, as a form of an integrated identity application that essentially creates a specific definition of a community. An integrated model may be easier to implement than a federated one due to the fact that an industry consortium could do so without having to pass any legislative or social initiatives. However, this would still be industry or application specific, so it has limitations insofar as to a community being willing to share its information on a broader basis.

Chapter 13

Can Threats Be Dealt with Effectively?

As mentioned earlier, there is no way of stopping all threats all the time. To even bridge the possibility of doing this would likely require a complete ground-up redesign of the entire global Internet-computing environment, along with every computing device. The intention of the redesign would be to maximize security at every point—software, devices, etc. But even with that, I would be willing to bet that with the best minds in the world doing the designing and building, the resulting system would still have to deal with people who could figure out, sooner or later, the means to compromise it. There is no fairy-tale security in the cards any time in the near or distant future. The huge investment in legacy systems, skills, and all of the elements that go into it, as well its intertwined existence with industry and society, means we just have to make what we have more secure; luckily, that is slowly happening. It's like the story of a person who upon their sixty-fifth birthday was asked how it felt to be that old. The person's answer was, "Not so bad, considering the alternative." So what we have in the global network, the Internet, is obviously, not so bad.

In fact, the global network has been and will continue to be a work in progress. With the origination of much of the technology taking place over a long period of time to get the net where it is today, it's safe to say there really was no way for anyone to have known, fifty or even ten years ago, what it could become. Considering the incremental nature of how technology is created, realistically there couldn't be a grand design to work towards. It has benefited from creeping incrementalism in all kinds of technology, and suffers from the same. Because of the looming sophistication of modern threats, it's time for more than incremental security improvement. There needs to be a leap in protection to address the years of accumulated weakness built into global computing protection technologies and methodologies.

A question that needs to be dealt with, like quality control on a manufacturing floor, is the following: When is the best time to fix a potential quality issue? Normally, that is as early in the production process as possible and certainly before the product comes off the production line. The implication here is the same. The difference is in implementation because the production line in this case is the overall network devices and applications, and the product is the data. This means that to ensure quality, any issues must be able to be contained before they can wreak havoc, which involves active protection against threats as well as dealing with product to reduce its exposure. As an avenue that is touched most by external and internal entities, as well as being a major storage site for data, the most prominent place to implement quality control mechanisms must begin at users and user endpoints.

As such, organizations have to establish security processes much like a production line, where if something looks out of whack, a line person (IT or some form of automation alarm) can stop the internal process for detailed analysis and, if appropriate, containment and immediate repair. Establishing a security intelligence and visualization ecosystem can help by applying rigorous analysis and testing for potential compromises before they induce an emergency or create a problem. Because there are many systems already in place that deliver a high level of quality data, now is the opportunity to take advantage of what they provide to improve intelligence quality. The results could be a leap ahead in protection capabilities against current threat actor sophistication, as they have continually taken advantage of the incrementally introduced protection weaknesses in technologies and methodologies developed and implemented in computing over decades.

Chapter 14

The Internet: Created for Sharing, Not Security

The Internet was originally designed to share documents between known parties more immediately and reliably than the methods of the time. The initial method to do this was to establish a connection between known parties and transfer a desired document between the cooperating users. In this scenario, users didn't have to go through any kind of particular rigor to verify another for an exchange between them. If there is already a known entity whether it's a direct or indirect relationship, who is requesting a document, most people would have no problem fulfilling the request. The point here is that the verification process—the need to ensure the safety of the information and the exchanging parties—wasn't designed into the system from inception or during any initial growth stage as the system became more common. The need for verification was something that has been added much later in the overall system's life cycle. The consequences are obvious and have reverberated through this community— now called the Internet—for the last twenty-five years.

Security from the Ground Up

Ideally, security needs to be a part of network and systems initial architectural design phase. This is happening in some areas and is an improvement from the recent past when it was treated as a bolt on, not as a part of a core operating environment. Even though this is better, overall security is still a layered approach and is not infused into the entire network environment. As movement is made to the IoE (Internet of Everything) incorporating so many other systems looks to be similar to the initial inception of network computing where security was an afterthought. This could introduce a whole host of new issues that could enhance threat actor options. To incorporate all these systems into an integrated protection scheme with a set of common APIs (Application Programming Interface) so they can easily be connected. The intended result of incorporating IoE into the environment of shared threat intelligence could be a broad sensor network that could provide valuable information to security systems. This could represent an interlocking of systems to help reduce or eliminate blind spots, making it easier for security and IT systems and staff to identify traffic sources and destinations of various device and network activities.

Visibility, intelligence gathering and assessment needs to enable a proactive threat protection stance and is derived from a foundation of these capabilities. This means that security systems must be carefully chosen for not only what they do individually, but as well as the information they provide for analysis and absorption into an overarching intelligence system. These systems will be less robust if they are just added on, as is more common today with layered silos. Most companies will need to scale their infrastructure for growth. If their overall architecture is a patchwork of security systems from the start it will just get uglier as their network grows.

Modern business, for over forty years, has come to expect computing resources to be in place as a part of standard operations from the beginning of the business. This means that the aspect of protecting systems must be a part of an organization's basic business plan and design. It needs to be core within the architecture of the overall system, processes, and methodologies during business's original formation.

Content and System Naming Conventions

It's notable how often we hear details on how a company got hacked, passwords stolen, and identities compromised. As you would expect, most successful hacks are often thought of as some wizard getting into an organization and delving into their systems with special code and techniques to identify all of the areas where crucial data is kept. If only it were so; unfortunately, the reality is a bit different. How many times has a hack been publicized where the victim company had all kinds of security in place, implying that the sophistication and capabilities of the hackers allowed them to bypass all of the protections to get, and stay, in the target organizations systems? Then as the story dies off of the front pages, the public starts getting a few more crucial details about what actually took place, and it often looks like this.

A successful hack of an organization can originate from many vectors because links and avenues to organizations are many and varied. A successful hacking case mentioned earlier came through an air-conditioning vendor link likely set up to submit proposals, e-mail communication, job scheduling, electronic billing and payments. The fact is any hack isn't magic on a hacker's part; but the result of target investigation and understanding of the overwhelming number of access points and amount of white-noise taking place in a targets environment. This is not an endorsement of hackers, but they must have a level of skill, persistence and luck to succeed.

To prevent unfortunate consequences of a successful hack, the design of a network specifically oriented toward application and data safety can help make unauthorized data access, identification and exfiltration more time consuming and difficult. Server, application, directory and file naming, location and storage conventions need to be designed to impose a significant time cost, increase attacker exposure and chance of detection. Many organizations with best of intentions set architectures up when they start that show elements of a protective structure. But often as they grow, it can get out of control, isn't rigorously enforced, or if seen as to restrictive individuals and departments figure out how to bypass its rules.

Active departmentalizing of data needs to be appropriate to its importance, along with application of enforcement policies and rules. This is where a well thought out layered defense can add value to security architecture. An organization could deploy a deeper serial defensive perimeter that would require a hacker to scale the defenses to get in as well as identify the site with the data they want, and require them to have to again scale the defenses to get out with any data. With centralized intelligence gathering applications and data stores would have priorities associated with their system and data value. Having a naming system that doesn't paint a huge red flag on servers, directories or files containing sensitive information would be a good place to start. Also managing non-IT and non-security staff so they don't try to circumvent naming convention policy is also crucial. Socially engineering this entire process to drive staff cooperation rather than the constant attempts at circumvention of policies is a much more effective approach than attempting to dictate something that can't be completely controlled no matter what you do. The reality is there is always someone who won't like a policy, no matter how good, concluding it's simply too much hassle to comply.

Chapter 15

Counter Moves

Retaliating

There have been many instances where retaliating against an attacker has been strongly considered for many good reasons. Unfortunately this kind of responsive activity has its own host of risks, none of which are particularly trivial. Any company can be 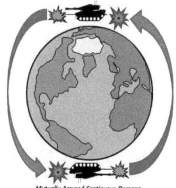 targeted by hackers that have determined the organization has something that they want. Or it could be a target company conducts an activity or represents a point of view, information, or attitude that runs counter to what a hacker thinks it should. Whether it's a state-sponsored or a commercial aggressor basically makes little

Mutually Assured Continuous Damage

initial difference to a targeted organization. Obviously there may be differences in the skill and time either may be able to apply to a target. In the overall picture this may a crucial element to how much damage can be done by a perpetrator. Either way, there is still a defense that an organization must maintain. Obviously, the resources hackers have can determine their success and how difficult it may be to either discover their presence, get them out, or determine what they have had access to once they're discovered. The hackers' perceived value of what they're after can impact the intensity and sophistication of an attack and can often be a strong influence as to how much time and resources hackers are willing to commit. Obviously, the more resources they have to conduct a hack may drive any potential reaction by them if they deem there is a retaliatory response from a target. In a retaliatory effort, giving that it would be difficult to have a clear idea of a hackers' resource base can make any kind of overt retaliation an even riskier endeavour. Attempting to retaliate or counterattack when one doesn't have knowledge of your opponent identity, or the resources they can apply, is a formula for disaster. It has been shown throughout history to be a game only a fool would pursue.

The issue is not whether one should or could retaliate. In fact, there are plenty of organizations with enough depth in staff capabilities, skill and system resources to deliver quite effective retaliatory strikes. The question is whether the benefit of doing so may even begin to come close to outweigh the risks it can bring. Retaliation can take many forms; some may have lower risks because they are indirect and not evident a target has taken an action, so they don't need to be overly concerned about a hacker response. This can include indirect actions such as blocking traffic from specific geographic areas (which is easy for a hacker to get around) to informing local or country government authorities who have the capacity to discover and thwart attacks with counter-responses tailored to a hacker. Doing this means the targeted organization isn't directly exposing itself to further retribution due to being seen as visibly retaliating.

Problems with a more obvious retaliation is it may set up a situation with potential that invokes continuous tit-for-tat responses between some external organization, with unknown resources, intention, and means, against an organization who in frustration took a shot at what they saw as the identified adversary. A risk is this could put the retaliating organization into a situation where it has to permanently assign staff and computing resources to an on-going skirmish, of which it would be difficult to ever determine an endpoint or conclusion with the hacker(s). As there is no set of rules for engagement between the parties, any end would not be up to the defender but determined by the external attacking group. For many reasons, that group may decide it's worth their effort to continue, or, for instance, use the game as a ruse to keep some of an organization's security staff engaged and then hit them from some other angle, such as through a less well-defended partner.

And, comparatively speaking, any organization that retaliates is generally a public entity and can more easily be tracked by their opponent. This puts their locations and resources in a much brighter spotlight than they could likely shine on any hacker. This makes a huge difference because an attacker can often keep from being tracked at all or certainly not as easily, as that is part of their modus operandi. Of course this makes it harder for an organization to see or predict a hacker's current or next action or even determine the focus of any action. It's like a person putting his or her hands up to stop an ocean wave—it may momentarily divert a little energy around their hands, but depending on the size of the wave, in the moments after the wave hits, the person's entire body would be engulfed in a swirling maelstrom of energy. And as the swirling continues, there would be no way for them to be able to tell exactly what direction the wave originally flowed from, or was going to. This could essentially turn a retaliating attempt into a tumbling body within the confusion of attacker's waves. And there would be little hope of floating to the top or even determining if or when the turbulence would subside. Unfortunately an organizations retaliation would most likely be a one sided battle, with the outcome not determinable by the organization.

Any individual or group of assailants can set up botnets to continually harass and impact organizations' resources. If a botnet is exposed and no longer available to a hacker, most likely they have others available, can hire resources from another hacker source, and continue to respond, if they wish. It may prove a temporary setback for them, but not to the level of public damage they may be able to inflict on an organization that has determined to visibly act as an adversary. This doesn't mean it can't work to hit back, but the risks are likely far higher today than the rewards.

An important question here would be, once started, how would an organization know that the assailant has given up or been beaten back? What criteria could be used to draw any kind of conclusion in either direction—whether one defeated an assailant or the assailant gave up and is targeting someone else? The fact is that no one could know this. That means once started, a target organization must assume that they may need to dedicate resources to a specific assailant, potentially without an end in sight.

Retaliation can take many forms, from active counterattacks against an aggressor to more duplicitous activities, such as honey pots that can seed an attacker with false information, hoping they conclude that they have penetrated their targets inner sanctum and got enough seemingly valuable information. The latter allows the target organization to also gather information on the attacker, their techniques, and hopefully the target information they are after. This can provide intelligence to building a defense based on what's learned in real-time about a perpetrators methodology and goals. This is a more benign form of retaliation, so it won't invoke any more response from the attacker other than their continued attempts to get around the new defenses to steal data versus attempting to specifically damage a target.

Also, an active retaliation must also consider possible unforeseen consequences. This could include potential damage to an organization from misidentifying an attacker that the organization retaliated against. If a hacker is retaliated against, they can set traps so that it might look like an attack came from a legitimate and innocent organization. This could create a situation where retaliation is mistakenly directed against a legitimate organization, creating serious damage to everyone involved. The legal, civil, ethical, and brand damage to either party could be significant, even more to the one taking the retaliatory action against an innocent bystander. If retaliation is exercised, the chance of this happening at some point is basically guaranteed; it's just a matter of when and who will be exposed based on a proactive policy of retaliatory behavior.

Industry and Government Consortium for Secure Computing

How can we manage and protect all the different kinds of information created and stored; personal and organization data along with resulting intelligence spawned from analysis, all while being able to safely access it? This has been an ongoing massive undertaking requiring a variety of remarkable resources to achieve both access and a level of security. The overall environment to secure data and make all its attendant variations and streams readily available while ensuring its security required today is too important to leave to so many anonymous methodologies and limited information sharing. There are too many competing interests, variations, use cases, methodologies and technologies within the giant map of world organizations. These all need to implement security coverage above a collage of solutions and provider organizations, even though every one of them may have respectable intentions to create effective solutions.

There are arrangements for cooperation between organizations demonstrated today. For instance an organization that can share malware and threat information between contributing organizations. This is a start but it needs to be broader. To extend this scope means a consortium of organizations; government, security and industry banded together in a mutual knowledge sharing and protection pact that can be accessible to members via a single clearing house. The intention would be help drive best practices and provide ready access to necessary threat information globally. As a single access point it could more quickly provide alerts or reports of issues, solutions, equally across the board to all members. It doesn't mean that every bit of information must be shared, such as an intellectual property reflected in algorithms for key security programs. It can mean access to organizations of all size to critical methodologies, information sharing on results of protection strategies, products, existing or new threats for everyone's benefit.

A vehicle to provide a consortium could be a membership funded organization that would act as a key gathering point for the best practices, establishing criteria for product effectiveness and a clearing house for up to date information and practices. This could be combined with a federated or integrated identity management ecosystem as well to help ensure the validity of individuals and organizations instead of the multiple leaky methodologies in play at thousands of organizations today. There could be a certain level of anonymity to allow organizations to protect what they consider their own proprietary processes, while simultaneously making aspects available to others through a contractual relationship any member of the consortium would have to adhere to.

Security and computing environments are just like biological systems; we all benefit if everyone is inoculated against contagion. Those organizations that wish to employ protection unique to their environment would benefit with a more actively shared security model, like other companies with whom they are connected and are known to have at least the same or a better level of protection. A sharing of best practices and other aspects so that one would expect a higher level of security across the board is, like inoculation, the only way for individual organizations to better ensure their own security.

A consortium is best not left to a single industry. Having it open to all would help avoid a situation where there might be a focus on advancing specific industries', companies' or governments own vested interests. This could also have branches to it, for instance members in specific industries may want to share any special needs or capabilities as well as gather input from other similar companies. To give it as broad an application and yet allow a certain level of focus would require an independent body funded by companies and government. It could have fees designed on a sliding scale so that start-ups or smaller companies would be able to join. This would better assure that at least a base level of "inoculation" as a requirement to be able to join the group in the first place.

An element that has been constantly battled out in various areas, including Congress and industry, is the need for a clear set of strictures that can finally address genuine concerns around personal information and data privacy. It's akin to madness to consider that so many companies having their own versions of data don't introduce all kinds of data conflict. A data clearing house could allow individual access to their own personal information, and could help make sure individuals are rigorously verified. Once verified, this system would help ensure that personal data continues to be accurate as mentioned in an earlier chapter.

A data clearing house, based on a level of subscription membership, would make selected data available for all members, relieving a multitude of organizations from the cost and risk of trying to keep private information up to date and protected. The clearing house would also maintain the verification of members to ensure information on the members was also up to date. There could be additional rules set so that a member could not be a conduit or source for a non-member to get information. At the same time, there ought to be a minimum threshold of knowledge and best practices shared across the board, to members and non-members alike. Again this would help set in place at least minimal inoculation for the entire population.

In the area of personal data, it could be subjected to tracking and control through the use of meta-tags with time stamps so that it could auto-delete at the end of a user's lifecycle for it. This would keep it so none is randomly floating about as is happening today. This could significantly reduce personal data-risk exposure by both reducing the time any data was outside of controlled environment, as well as limiting it to vetted members. And meta-tags would allow it to be trackable, so if some kind of breach took place, it has a better chance of being traced back to the organization that checked it out. Obviously the meta-tags and data are encrypted so that the information couldn't be changed by anyone, whether the data were stolen or inside of a trusted environment.

Chapter 16

Moving Forward

Addressing the state of security today starts with accepting where we are and then determining what is necessary to move forward. It really can't stay "business as usual" since it struggles to provide the overall active visibility and intelligence necessary to deal with active attacks in use today. To move forward doesn't mean throwing out what's already in place; in fact, whether it has gaps or not, there is a level of commitment to existing technology and processes because there has been a level of success. The problem is the lower level of overall ability against the intelligence that is brought to bear in modern attacks. Tearing everything out and replacing it just isn't an option. What we would be left with in the interim would be a disaster. At the same time, there is a threshold that needs to be overcome as to what our systems can deliver today versus what they need to be able to deliver in the immediate future.

The recognition of the computing environment's complexity and the difficulty of trying to protect valuable data clearly have many issues. Trying to apply a broader approach instead of constantly trying to patch holes, producing yet more silo products and skills that are only applicable in a single area, can't address the whole picture. Being able to broadly see and specifically investigate and apply intelligence designed to take out the blind speed bumps our current environment continually throws in the path of effective security is key.

The fact is that human beings are the threat actors—not systems, malware, or viruses—but people actively trying to steal anything of value, utilizing sophisticated systems and tools. This people problem needs to be dealt with by people, using tools that allow them to be as proactive in their protection as the attacks are proactive in their assaults. A proactive defense requires a broad overall view of endpoints, applications, systems, and their activity as well as being able to dive deeply into any area as the need arises. Visibility should enable proactive hunting for issues and threats into any instance, without notifying or alerting an attacker as a key part of a vibrant defense. This should allow specific inspection and analysis of incidents that may be unique within an organization or its industry so that security personnel can rigorously investigate their systems. The purpose would be to see if there is anomalous or suspicious behavior that may be present but has not triggered any notifications.

All this translates into fundamental, but not so easy, tasks to do for maximizing security flexibility against any threat actor or activity. For instance, research presented by Gartner[44] indicates that 70 percent to 90 percent of malware found today in breach investigations is unique. These unique pieces of malware represent a part of an attack-event chain in virtually every security incident.[45] As mentioned, the fact that the malware is unique most of the time means it's a human being on the other side of the attack, tuning, adjusting, and changing the attack to address the defenses identified at a target. The systems and software is not the attacker; these are just the tools, not the cause of the attack. It's the variability from the human threat actor(s) utilizing various tools, creating challenging vectors of attack that must be defended against.

Many of today's traditional security systems, well-designed and coded following rigorous standards, aren't as effective as needed against the human actors that are behind a successful breach.

---

[44] Gartner Security and Risk Management Summit June 8-11 2015 National Harbor
[45] Verizon 2015 Data Breach Investigations Report

And with all of their activity, may confuse or create a false sense of security. As previously mentioned, it may even be more difficult to be secure because the number of deployed systems at any site can generate millions of events and messages, creating confusion as well as misunderstanding about threats.

Today's type of systems are more like a police officer who spots someone in the act of committing a crime. It's pretty straightforward to stop the process and subsequently remove the nuisance and the threat from the street. In that type of instance, police can contain the pettier criminals, keeping them at bay and in line for everyone's protection. However, when an incident has already happened, and you aren't sure what happened as no one was there to witness it, that's when those who can reconstruct an incident, such as detectives, are brought in. These professionals can conduct forensic analysis, essentially building an intelligence base to provide context as they inspect, and analyze the evidence available. They will review the physical evidence, psychological and social aspects to determine the different actions taken in order to reconstruct the event and determine the facts and sequence of what happened surrounding and up to the event. The detective builds his or her knowledge base surrounding the entirety of the incident to understand it. This is in contrast to looking at an incident as though nothing before or after it had happened or may be relevant to it. There is always a before and after for any incident, the need is to understand the incident and timelines of activity.

If, for example, an attacker has been testing an organizations defense, a trail will be left. This trail is part of the organizations intelligence base and can be a map regarding the attackers continuous activities. This could allow defenders to see how they can adapt a defense against an event that is more than a single point. For instance this is identifying all the points before, during and after an attack whether or not it was able to bypass a defense.

Active Forensics

Before, during, and after are crucial telling points for understanding and adapting a defense against active players. Older-style systems, such as AV, IDS/IPS, firewalls, URL filtering, and the vast majority of security systems, are based on something they knew at one time. And even as they get constant updates to their knowledge base of past events, these are still past events. These don't build enough intelligence to help human defenders to make the adjustments essential to a proactive defense against proactive attacks. This is much like the policeman arriving just after a crime has been committed. Because no one saw it as it took place; the only evidence is the result of the crime, not its progression.

This is where digital detectives need to ply their trade, and their contribution can be realized in a number of different ways. For instance, they can re-enact any incident in a number of different ways to lock down exactly what led up to it and took place immediately afterwards. In a sense it's like ongoing penetration testing to find vulnerabilities an attacker can exploit. An organization could apply a level of continuous and contained sweeps of various parts of a network to be able to find anything of suspicion or unusual nature without a hacker being able to detect or interfere with the internal snooping process.

Even though it's important, penetration testing is still looking at the past. What it does is based on what it knows about a network environment with deployed versions of systems and software. And, even if a vulnerability is found it can take time, sometimes a long time, for an organization to apply a patch to fix it. This is where security has to step beyond the known and be able to use the techniques of a detective. A difference is this is not only to do forensics of a known event, but also to conduct forensics of potentials—to hunt through a network and look for activity that may point to some type of negative event or something that could be exploited by a hacker. The basis of this is to understand techniques—those steps and processes that need to happen for a successful attack to take place.

Any security system can gather useful information; however, quite often, it doesn't know it's useful because it doesn't fit into a category that it can use to determine a threat. So often, the information is lost to the overall environment. If another security system had seen a particular snippet of information, they may have been able to correlate it against other snippets of information, for a more complete picture to take action. Having the ability to proactively link up, correlate, and assess existing information is a key step in developing intelligence. This means analysts and incident responders must be able to use all information elements to incorporate it within complete time lines to act as a forensic detective.

The purpose is to create a more dynamic view within a network, its servers, applications, endpoints, and any device. The human analyst should be able to assess systems information as indicators to determine any relevance and follow the trail to deduce implications. This knowledge chain should help an analyst or an incident researcher determine potential meaning in what they're looking at; is it a threat? If so, a threat to what, where has it been, how did it get in, and what specific activity is it currently conducting or trying to conduct? This whole exercise should help to determine the source of an event and, based on being able to run the code for instance in a protected sandbox, assess what a threat actor may be trying to do. A purpose would be to help establish information as to where a threat actor may be located, which can indicate whether a commercial or state actor. Also whether you've seen their work pattern before, and if there are any associations that can be made with other activity taking place within your network. Based on what the hacker is doing, an analyst can get an idea as to whether the threat actor is financially motivated—is it specifically money or information that can be turned into money? This can help establish what would be likely internal targets they're after. When working with security partners, the information on the hacker's path can be one that indicates a particular player, such as pointing to a state actor who likely has far different intentions and time lines to accomplishing their task.

Who the threat actor may be is information that can have a significant impact on what one does to defend the network and information. Based on what is found out about a threat impacts if one may want or need to involve a third party for assistance. Whatever the information discovered is used as part of an intelligence baseline to continually build a threat protection information base. Then, if something takes place, the defender has a starting point to hopefully more quickly identify and create a response to an assailant. This could enhance the ability for response agility and speed in understanding an event and attacker and assemble a defense or plug a weakness. If previously set up, redirecting an attack into a honeypot to gather information about it could have immense value.

A New Model: Internal Counterintelligence

When I refer to counterintelligence, I'm using the term as described in Wikipedia. Obviously, we have to accept that in industry, there are a few areas of counterintelligence that won't apply to how industry conducts it. In a pretty long definition, Wikipedia refers to counterintelligence as information gathered and activities conducted to protect against espionage,[46] other intelligence activities, sabotage, or assassinations conducted for or on behalf of foreign powers, organizations or persons or international terrorist activities, but not including personnel, physical, document or

---

[46] This refers to a government and company/firm or individual obtaining information considered secret or confidential without the permission of the holder of the information

communications security programs. For our purposes, I think we can safely assume there will be little to worry about around the area of assassinations, even if there may be an occasional fantasy in this regard about an assailant. That is thankfully out of our domain. It is safe to say that protecting against espionage, sabotage, and other intelligence activities that compromise an organizations systems, data, bank account or staff is fair game.

Every organization has the right to defend itself and its items of value, and to take reasonable actions in order to do so. Being able to learn about your adversary and apply proactive or responsive changes to protect against any assailant activities is a fair and prudent approach. To do this means that there must be an application of tools and skilled individuals in order to understand current environment by conducting thorough investigation and analysis of it. Based on this deep knowledge of a current state, they can then evaluate potential avenues of risk and be able to outline appropriate defensive postures. This requires intelligence, visibility, and the simple acceptance that to keep a fire from your domain means you have to properly prepare and being able to adjust to the vagaries of a particular or series of events.

Counterintelligence does not mean counterattack. In this context, it means being able to institute a proactive defense that's based on broad and deep knowledge of your entire network environment. No one wants to be held hostage by an attacker because it's easy for them to first penetrate and then move about with impunity. Getting out of that position requires constant visibility and the capacity for vigilance. That means if one is to have security silos of information, then you must be able to make use of that information instead of losing it to the noise of the network. The static silo systems need to be incorporated within the practice scope for analysts or incident responders to review and analyze device and application activities. And this continuous exercise needs to be inclusive within the entire network environment. Being able to model what a threat may be trying to do, again within the entire system, is a scope of investigation and analysis that should add to an organization's threat intelligence aptitude. The investigative environment would allow an investigator to work at a pace that is appropriate to the situation. This means being able to investigate a specific threat without further risk of contamination to other systems so they can adapt their defense as needed.

The information available for deeper analysis already exists in a variety of products. The problem is for a human defender to be able to get to it and then make sense of it and any implications it may point to. This can be specific such as searching for a known IOC (Indicator of Compromise, an industry term) to see if an IOC exists on any device. Or to investigate without any specific indicator means a researcher must have some concept and means of what to look for with tools that allow them to do the level of search and investigation appropriate to a situation.

Dynamic Protection: Historic and Forward-Looking Investigative Forensics

By visibility, I mean proactive visibility into a system's past and current events and activities. This requires what has been considered historical forensics, such as the detective rebuilding the crime scene to find out what happened. In the digital world, this also means looking at activities in the past to see if there is anything currently present or executed on a device in the past that can imply something today. And, as mentioned earlier, this means the ability to look forward. Not into the future per se, but based on what should be on a device, what are its activities outside normal activity, or are there questionable external communication. For instance, one may ask if a Window's registry may have changed and why, where a specific executable ran, and what it may be trying to do. If there is an incident identified from a past event, did it spawn other events and what were they trying to do? This gets into areas such as a lateral movement inside of an organizations network, or an action that may be reaching out to an external server (*Command and Control* or CnC, or C2). And, if anything is identified, an investigator should be able to trace it out, whether from a set of historical tracks or tracing out something currently active. Even though initially a piece of code or executable may seem benign at first, upon further investigation, it may reveal its true design is not conducive to the organizations security.

Investigation and Analysis

The purpose of being able to historically and proactively discover and identify issues is to give organization the tools and methodologies for a more flexible security environment. To be effective, any security environment has to be as flexible as the threat actors it deals with. It's fine to have a level of faith that static systems are good enough to stop a level of threats, but hoping for more than that against highly skilled professionals is misplaced faith. The countermove to deal with this reality today lies with skilled human beings and tools that balance the defenses capabilities with the offense of today, not what it was ten years ago. The result should be an additive intelligence base going forward that can be used to dynamically adjust defenses against any type of attack methodology and style as its taking place, and for future similar attempts.

Counterintelligence for the Masses

Visibility, investigation and analysis combined with traditional security static capabilities is a basis for a security ecosystem that allows far more adaptability to dealing with existing and a changing threat landscape. Part of it could utilize automation where it makes sense. At the same time network, device and application visibility gives analysts the environment needed to recognize elements of an emerging incident, not after it's already struck. Being able to look between-the-cracks to find hidden or suspicious activity or files goes a long way to addressing the design gaps of traditional static systems. A security ecosystem needs flexible techniques and methods to defend against new threats. And it can do this by giving every security professional a broader picture of the environment they're in as well as a view into the actions and techniques they're working against. Part of this includes internal intelligence-threat gathering that can take all of the scattered internal security data and pull out the relevant information to an organization. Pulling out the gems is at the forefront of visibility and intelligence; whether past incidents, current activities, elements that may be suspicious, wrapped together, give security professionals the tools to do the job they are hired for—protecting the content that runs all of our lives, however banal or illustrious that content may be.

Moving Forward, Dynamic Visibility, and the Utilization of Threat Intelligence

There will never be a perfect answer to the issues facing all of us in the utilization of complex systems and tools to secure information. It doesn't matter whether it's the person who just uses systems to get a job done and doesn't need to know what's taking place outside that job. Or whether it's a person who provides the operational systems, access, and data protection. Ideally everyone desires to have what they need to excel at their job, as well as be comfortable and safe in their computing endeavors.

A significant area to address is the aspect of ownership of personal data. This is foundational to how protection, storage, access, and utilization of the data and systems are dealt with within a protection sphere. Right now, this is a series of Pandora's boxes that one never knows what they will get when opened. However, once opened, it's difficult, if not impossible, to close as its opening leads to a chain of events that are difficult to detect or determine their behavior.

Again, it breaks down to visibility and intelligence; which, in essence, is high-definition security visibility. If security continues in the same direction as it has been going for years, it will only get harder to implement and maintain, thus less effective as attackers continue to get better at their game.

Other areas important to consider for a complete picture going forward include the following:

- No person, company, technology, or combination thereof can completely stop all threats.

- In dealing with a threat and breaches, like good quality control that manufacturers use when producing a product, it's best to address the issue (threat) as close to its origination as possible. That point is its entry point, which is generally a user endpoint. The reason for this is that the deeper a threat gets into a network, the more difficult it is to find and eradicate.

- Not all data is created equal, so don't expend the same resources for every bit of data or systems. A foundation for protecting information first and foremost is to establish proper information logistics with well-defined classification of all information. This includes defining appropriate locations for information based on this classification, something organizations must fashion from their beginning, and adjust as needed and enforce rigorously as their network grows.

- It's critical to ensure that data is properly treated and that limited resources aren't wasted protecting information or systems beyond the scope of their value. If all information is treated as critical, then none of it's critical. If organizations have to spread their protection capabilities too thinly across systems to protect information that doesn't warrant the effort, then they are crippling their defenses. This should include exercising protection for important data that includes encrypting it both in a stored state as well as in transit.

- Based on the continuous exposure to threats organizations are subjected to, they need to have tools that provide visibility into the entire network and all its devices. They must be able to continually investigate any and all activity taking place at any endpoint. This includes within their network core, on servers as well as application and connection points within their network, and must include partners and any other external entry point.

- Eventually, an attacker will get in. The goal is being not only able to detect something rapidly, but to also inspect and analyze any activity. This is so when something does get past edge protection systems, they can be found and stopped. Organizations must be able to apply threat intelligence pervasively across every point in a network. This means not just the core but also to continually interrogate endpoints, so that active threat identification can take place everywhere at any time.

- Being able to analyze threat data within the context of big data, using machine learning and predictive analytics about threats or suspicious issues, are capabilities that need to be at the bidding of security professionals. Visibility comes from delivering to analyst's information presented in various ways to permit them to determine how the information may pertain to a threat. This mean an analyst has to have the tools to follow any appropriate event and the ability to search along various avenues and investigate across an entire network, end to end.

People and systems need to address the threats of today and tomorrow by enabling professionals to see into all their traffic, applications, and devices. This activity must be able to create a layer of visibility to quiet the noise and debris created in a normal network that hackers utilize to their advantage. It needs to help the security analysts up their game, make them smarter, and clear away the fog of incidents so that they can continually step over all the unintended and intended obstructions.

Wrapping this up, there is no such thing as a final, uber-security system that can take every feed from all systems, mix it all together, and come out with miracle answers and the immediate ways of dealing with each threat. There is really no way to build this, even though it's been tried in many areas. Unfortunately, SIEMs don't turn the data they get into intelligence about threats that may be related to any incidents or events. And, when you consider on larger networks how much data, logs, events, can pass through it overall, it's understandable that a SIEM has not solved the problem regarding what to do with all this information..

So, intelligence building within a sphere of visibility has to be an ongoing incremental effort. Today, the main goal should be to use visibility to help assemble a threat intelligence baseline, that can be shared internally and externally as needed.

The point is that today's layer after layer of multiple complex systems and consoles must be reexamined in a wholesale fashion. Clearly it has worked to a significant level, and simple reality is we can't throw it all away. There needs to a methodology for reviewing the return from adding another security product to conclude whether it's actually less than the price of complexity it may introduce.

There is a tipping point where security actually starts to get in its own way and essentially reduces the very security it's trying to provide. Whether it's a product, process, or methodology, it's critical to stay below that tipping point because it actually makes us all more vulnerable. This must include better methodology and shared resources, such as cloud access to global threat intelligence with connectivity everywhere so that no system is an isolated unprotected computing point.

It's clear that there is enough intelligence, experience, and expertise available to move in this direction. We have to realize that we can't just rely on technology to plug every gap. The technology has to support the social process of humans, within the scope of their everyday activity, utilizing technology as appropriate to an organizations immediate social constructs. This also means that there needs to be humans, with the right skills and tools that can see, at any time and under any circumstances, exactly what is going on within their overall domain.

This won't arrive because an organization can design the next great product or algorithm for machine learning or artificial intelligence, expecting it to spot and stop any and all threats. That doesn't mean we can't get better, but the fact is that so will our adversary; they, too, can build tools as well to increase their capabilities and skill. Security really must be a world body of organizations with a higher level of cooperation and sharing. Continuing to have directions defined based on who can plug the latest hole in some application or operating system, or create a new product that covers a gap that is found in existing security products, isn't a strategy. Security companies, governments, and commercial organizations can make up a conglomeration of mutually interested partners, and work together to establish baselines we can all live with, not the ad-hoc manner of today.

The goal is to make security easier for those who are at risk and are the entry points for every hack—people on endpoint devices. This is as much a social gap in the use of technology as it is a technology gap through a technologies misapplication. Including aspects of human nature and social structure that can be applied by professionals, who design, deploy, and support security is a mix that needs to be addressed. Without this recognition, all we continue to do is patch one hole after another. As we do that, the threat actors continue to poke holes in the rigid walls we've built.

Humans, their social structures, and technology are adaptable creatures. Using them together, versus over-reliance on technology, could allow security to better fit into the human social structure instead of acting as though it can stand outside of it. Consequently, this method will provide a better structure to protect our information. The fact is that the social constructs we live within, whether as a user or a security professional, is better protected if we understand the protection is not just against a machine and some software, but humans, their intelligence and technology within a global and local social structure.

Glossary

Advanced Threats: Today's breed of cyberattacks that are designed to be difficult to detect by signature-based security defenses.

Advanced Persistent Threat (APT): A sophisticated cyberattack that utilizes advanced stealth techniques to remain undetected for extended periods of time.

Advanced Targeted Attack (ATA): Another name for advanced persistent threat.

Attack Surface: The sum of all the exploitable systems exposed to external threat as well as vulnerabilities, whether known or unknown, that exists within hosts and devices on a given network.

Authentication: The process of verifying the identity of a user, computer, or service.

Backdoor: Malware that enables an attacker to bypass normal authentication mechanisms to gain unauthorized access to a system or application.

Baiting: A social engineering attack in which physical media (such as USB stick) containing malware is purposely left in the vicinity of a targeted organization.

Blended Threat: Cyberattack that combines multiple attack techniques in one effort to penetrate a target computing system

Bot: An infected computer, whether endpoint or server, that is centrally controlled by an unauthorized command-and-control (CnC) server and generally part of a botnet (also known as a Zombie).

Bot-Herder: The owner who controls a botnet.

Botnet: A broad network of bots working together.

Bootkit: Malware that is a variation of a rootkit and often used to attack an encrypted hard disk.

BYOD (Bring Your Own Device): An organizational policy that allows employees to utilize personally owned devices to access the organization's data.

Cloud Threat Intelligence Network: An Internet-based service used to distribute cyberattack intelligence to customers and receive data from them to update the intelligence base.

Command-and-Control System (CnC): A server operated by a cybercriminal to provide instructions to bots.

Correlation Engine: Aggregation of information and determining the relationship between multiple data streams from devices and software to help identify security issues and risks.

Cybercriminal: An individual or groups of individuals who utilize hacking techniques to illegally steal data from target organization's computers for personal or state gain.

Cyberterrorism: The use of Internet-based attacks as a part of terrorist activities with deliberate actions to disrupt a target's computing network.

Cyberwar: Politically motivated hacking to conduct sabotage and/ or espionage against a nation state.

Data Loss Prevention (DLP): A system designed to prevent potential data loss based on patterns of the data, such as social-security or credit-card numbers.

Data Integrity: The accuracy and consistency of information during its creation, transmission, and storage.

Defense-in-Depth or Security Layering: A strategy that relies on the deployment of a series of cybersecurity defenses so a threat that may have been missed by one layer may be caught by another.

Distributed Denial of Service Attack (DDoS or DoS): An attack intended to disrupt or disable a target's computing services by flooding it with benign communication requests that overwhelm its ability to respond to legitimate communications.

Drive-by-Download: Software, often malware that is downloaded onto a computer from the Internet without the user's knowledge or permission.

Endpoint: A point where data is either manipulated or stored. User endpoint is the same, except this endpoint is generally in the control of an individual user.

Exfiltration: An unauthorized release of data or files from within a computer system or network.

False Negative: When a system misclassifies a file containing malware as benign.

False Positive: When a system misclassifies a benign file as malware.

Hacktivism: The use of computing systems as a means to protest and/or promote political goals.

Intrusion Detection System (IDS): An out-of-band system that monitors for known signatures and alerts when one may be detected.

Intrusion Protection System (IPS): An inline (active) system that monitors network traffic for signatures and blocks based on the detection of a certain signature.

Keylogger: An application that can record user keystrokes on any system in which it is installed.

Logic Bomb: A program that performs a malicious function when a predetermined set of circumstances occurs.

Malware: A general category of malicious software, such as virus, worm, or Trojan, that is created to disrupt a computer's normal operation for a hacker to gain access to protected systems and to gather sensitive information.

Multi-Stage Attack: A cyber-attack that incorporates multiple types of malware that are designed to be launched at different phases as part of an advanced attack.

Multi-Vector Attack: A cyber-attack designed to target multiple hosts within the same organization by utilizing several attack techniques.

Patch: A vendor-supplied software update to correct vulnerability in applications or an operating system.

Patch Management: The cyclical process of acquiring, testing, and installing patches to computer systems in a coordinated manner to address vulnerabilities.

Phishing: The act of sending an e-mail that falsely claims to be legitimate in order to trick a user into surrendering private information, such as credit card or social security numbers.

Rootkit: Malware that provides privileged, root-level access to a computer.

Spear Phishing: A phishing attempt that is specifically directed toward an organization or a person within that organization.

Spyware: A type of malware that collects information about users without their knowledge or permission.

State-Sponsored Threat Actor: Cybercriminals that are employed and directed by nation-states to conduct cyberattacks against targets of that state for politically motivated purposes.

Trojan: Malware that masquerades as a legitimate file or helpful application with the ultimate purpose of helping a hacker gain unauthorized access to a computer.

Whaling: A cyberattack that is directed specifically at senior executives or other high-profile targets within an organization.

Worm: A form of malware that exploits network vulnerabilities and can normally replicate itself across networks and devices without human intervention.

Vulnerability Scanning: Software systems that are designed to assess computer and network infrastructure devices and software for vulnerabilities and misconfigurations that expose them to attack.

Zero-Day Attack: A cyberattack against a currently unknown (or unreported) vulnerability in operating systems, applications, or other core computing systems before the vulnerability is either known or has been applied.

Dan Reis has spent more than twenty-five years in the technology field in Silicon Valley. He was director of product marketing at Nokia Internet Security and director of product marketing at Trend Micro. He is currently the director of product marketing for a leading cyber intelligence company. He has earned a bachelor's degree in economics, an MBA, and a master's degree in information systems security.

www.ingramcontent.com/pod-product-compliance
Lightning Source LLC
LaVergne TN
LVHW042333060326
832902LV00006B/148